Foreword

When the opportunity arose to be associated with 'Where
to Go in Greece', we were particularly delighted. Trevor
Webster has produced a very readable book packed not
only with practical information about Greece and her
islands, but also with the sort of personal observations
that add that special dash of flavour.

As the leading holiday company operating in Greece, we
recognise the need for detailed information and guidance
for the would-be traveller. Here at last is a book, covering
over 70 islands, which answers all the questions, written in
the impartial and highly personal style of someone who
knows and loves this unique country.

Whether you are a committed Grecophile or a potential
first-timer, we are sure you will find this book invaluable
in helping you to plan your next holiday to Greece.

Thomson Holidays

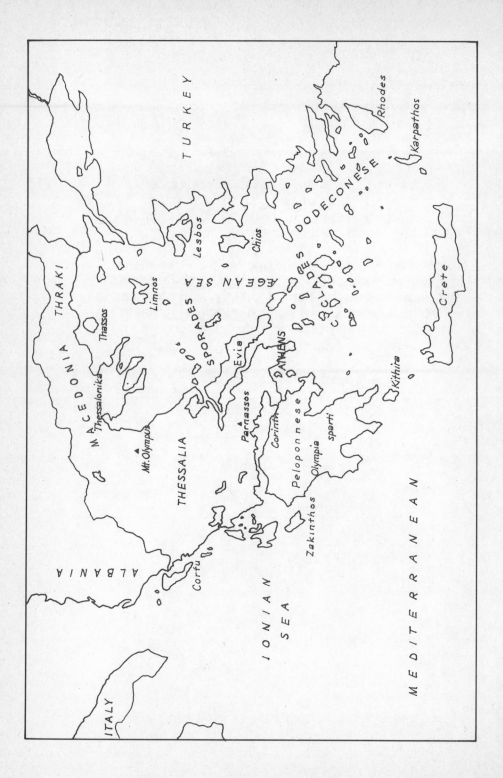

WHERE TO GO
IN
GREECE

THOMSON HOLIDAY
COLOUR EDITION

SETTLE and BENDALL (WIGMORE)

© 1985 Trevor Webster
All rights reserved. No part of this publication
may be reproduced or transmitted in any form or
by any means without permission.
First published by Settle and Bendall (Wigmore)
32 Savile Row
London W1X 1AG

ISBN (Hardback) 0 907070 24 8
     (Paperback) 0 907070 25 6

Printed by Villiers Publications Ltd
Ingestre Road, London NW5 1UL

Contents

The Magic of Greece

In the early sixties Greece was an unusual place to holiday. People who favoured Majorca, or France, or didn't go abroad, often asked what was so special about Greece. The easy answer was that it was hot, cheap and friendly.

In the late sixties Greece became 'that new place'. And, despite the rule of the colonels, many people gave it a try and liked it. In the early seventies it was the place for 'a beach of your own' and the tourist influx swelled from the hundreds of thousands into the millions. Nowadays, it is no longer a new place, but you can still find a beach – possibly 1,000 beaches or even an island – to yourself. Thanks to the islands, Greece boasts the longest coastline in Europe. In the much-travelled world of the eighties that should be enough to explain the lure of the country, but there is more.

Greece is the cradle of history. It is where most of our childhood myths began, where poetry, imagination and wisdom combined to speculate about the origins of man and gods. It is also where reason raised its pretty head and where concepts like freedom, democracy and happiness were first debated and recorded by serious scribes. You can prove that Egypt and Mesopotamia were lands of sophisticated culture centuries before Agamemnon led a united Greek army into Asia to rescue Helen of Troy. But, where is their spirit today? In their pyramids and the ziggurats we can honour them, but not in philosophy, mathematics, astronomy and literature. Nor in the words that make up our language, our hymns and our culture. Some speak of Alexander and some of Hercules, but few of brave Lysander and the countless Ptolemies . . .

Greece is still hot, cheap and friendly. It is the hottest country in Europe, with the southern isles and Peloponnese on the same meridian as north Africa. Most areas record 300 days' sunshine a year, with a mild dry climate from March to November.

So far it is cheaper than any country in the Common Market. Don't look at the terms on the door of a package tour hotel, or the price of drinks in its smart bar, but at the price of meat, fruit and vegetables in the local market. Or at the price of wine and food in a small quayside restaurant. While the pound buys around 180 drachmas, you can have a bottle of retsina on the table for 40p, and the most expensive wine you can find in 90 per cent of restaurants will be £2. A bottle of beer is about 40p and it is hard to spend more than £4 or £5 on a meal out for two.

Small hotels and rooms in island homes come remarkably cheap, too. The standard price for a double room on a small island is still between 600 and 1,200 drachmas, and you can often beat down the price in off-season. The same low prices also apply to internal travel. Travelling round Greece by bus, plane, train or boat costs less than half what it would for the same distance in Britain.

Greece remains friendly in spite of itself. The march of tourism, at once the saviour and spoiler of the country, is having some curious effects on traditional Greek hospitality towards strangers. There is a get-rich-quick mentality spreading through the main tourist areas but, as yet, it hasn't killed off the natural exuberance of the small beach tavernas, nor the genuine smile of welcome from the donkey-borne peasant.

Greece is exotic, close to nature and visually exciting. Although the cradle of history and culture, it has the allure of the primitive. It is the nearest thing in Europe to the mystic east, a stepping stone to Asia.

This comes alive through a crystal haze-free light. It is possible not only to see a long way, but to see objects in sharp relief. This light can also be harsh and cruel. It highlights dross, lack of taste and neglect of the environment, which are all too evident in Greece. But, at night look up at the brilliant stars and moon, shining without any challenge from artificial light or pollution.

Greece is easy to get to, easy to live in, and divinely quiet in places.

There is an informality about the country that you find nowhere else in Europe. Outside of casinos and smart hotels, you can wear what you like. You can lunch in a swim suit and don't have to worry whether your hair is combed, clothes pressed or room tidy. It all helps in a break from the buzz-saw modern world. So does the primitiveness of the country. Curiously, for a land where people rarely speak in a whisper, where children learn to shriek as soon as walk, and where drivers seem to use their horns more than their steering wheels, you can find endless oases of peace, untouched by time and progress.

There are islands where there is no traffic, TV or even clocks that work. You can time travel to the 19th Century or even the Middle Ages. Sleep like the sleeping beauty, woken only by the waves, goat bells, a chorus of cicadas, or the braying of a donkey.

If there was one word alone that explains the appeal of Greece, it is 'isichia'. It means peace and quiet and that would draw me back even if all the rest was an empty dream.

Choosing a Holiday

When to go

The crowds arrived in the 1970's when Greece was successfully promoted as 'the place', where you would have a beach to yourself. Now, it has reached the point where the tiny nine million population is almost equalled by tourists – and over half of them go in July and August.

If you are planning a trip to Greece in July or August, especially late July or early August, take plenty of sun cream, a tube of insect repellant and a hat. If you go without booking, a light sleeping bag might be a useful optional extra especially on major tourist islands. This is high season, and it can be both uncomfortably hot and crowded these days. August has an additional hazard. The meltemmi wind blows hardest across the Aegean during the month and, though it can cool the nights marvellously, it can also make swimming and lying on a beach a lot less pleasant.

The heat beckons alluringly to refugees from an English summer, but it is too easy to forget that most of Greece is on a level with North Africa. So, don't throw yourself upon Apollo's altar as a burnt sacrifice, especially if the meltemmi is blowing hard and disguising the full blast of the furnace. The temperature is probably around 92 degrees in the sheltered shade. You can feel it well enough later that night when you lie turning on the spit in bed.

The Greek Tourist Office are now curbing their straightforward promotion efforts because they are worried that there are not enough beds for visitors in July and August. Hence their recent campaign to spread tourists through the year by advertising the undisputed charms of the Greek spring and autumn, and across the areas of the country that are not so popular. Witness the money and promotion devoted to Halkidiki. Both campaigns have great intrinsic merit, but if you have to go in July or August because of school holidays, try to make it early July or late August and be prepared for a few problems with accommodation if you haven't already booked any. Hence my suggestion of carrying a light sleeping bag for spending a night on a beach or the deck of a ship between islands.

The best months of the year, to combine heat and perfect weather with a civilised choice of accommodation and more of the true Greek atmosphere are June and September. June is less crowded and the countryside is a blaze of flowers, but the sea is warmer in September. June has the first flush of hot weather fruit – strawberries, peaches and apricots. September has the grape season, figs and succulent melons.

May and October come close on all these counts, especially late May and early October. The weather is usually warm, particularly in the south Aegean; everywhere is less crowded; prices tend to fall or be negotiable. May has an abundance of flowers and the feel of a hot English summer. The sea stays warm through October.

November, December, March and April are ideal for people who want to flee the tourists, but still see the sites. They resemble good English spring or September weather. You can swim without discomfort in a swimming pool and even in the sea around mid-day through November and December. March and April have the added bonus of the Greek Easter festivals, when every church sparkles with flowers and music, and the awakening countryside mirrors the celebrations, with nature bursting into bloom everywhere.

The winter months of November to April are less warm, but still sunny and delightfully uncrowded. In January and February Greece experiences something of a winter with snow falling on the mountains in the north, and Mount Parnassus becomes one of the sunniest ski resorts in Europe.

Package Tour

With over 150 British tour operators now offering holidays in Greece, a package deal is often the first and obvious thing to think of when planning your Greek visit. The Greek National Tourist Office (address page 62) issues an extremely helpful booklet listing all current British tour operators. This comes complete with details of where each company goes to in Greece and what type of holiday they offer.

Hotels, villas and tavernas are the mainstay of all holiday programmes, and you will find a wide choice both in type of accommodation and destination. There will be something, somewhere, to suit every Greek holiday taste. Just beware of being landed in a place that's dull and uncharming – like a hotel on the Athenian Riviera, sandwiched between the airport and noisy coastal motorway and where you might have to pay a high premium for drinks and snacks in a bar which has you as a captive audience.

Fly-drive holidays give you maximum flexibility as to where you go, stop, swim, and stay and for how long. They are ideal for seeing a lot of the mainland or a big island like Crete in a short time. But, it is costly to take a car to the smaller islands, other than short ferry hops, and you may well find you feel bound to travel tiring distances to get value from your car.

You may fancy a cruise as an easy way to see many islands without having to plan, organise, or wonder where to go. You can use it as a pilot venture, noting any places you particularly like on the way, for a longer visit next year. A cruise ticket also buys you an instant family of friends. But, cruising is expensive – upwards of £450 – most passengers are past middle age

and you have to settle for a few hours ashore in places where you might like to settle for a few days.

For the younger age group, yachting and flotilla holidays are becoming increasingly popular. In your small craft, you can get to isolated coves and beaches whither no other tourists fly. You can also get quite a sense of adventure, especially if you hit choppy seas and the rest of the flotilla is heading over the horizon.

Your own Odyssey

Athens is 1,500 miles from London and a journey of 3½ hours by air. Take off half an hour for Corfu, add half an hour for Crete, Kos or Rhodes.

It takes three days or more by coach, rail or car diagonally across Europe or via the heel of Italy. That journey used to be worth doing when it cost half as much as the airfare, and you were as eager to see Rome, Venice or Munich, as Athens and the Greek islands. It is hard to justify now because air fares have crashed in price relative to sea and rail travel. The magic carpet provided by the charter airlines is the obvious way to travel, unless you have weeks to spare and don't mind braving three days in a coach. Once in Greece how you travel around depends on your age, pocket and inclination.

The best way for my money, remains the way of the heroes – a wandering odyssey, searching for the perfect place. Travel light and take advantage of modern transport. There are regular cheap buses across the mainland, regular cheap ships to most islands and regular, relatively cheap, planes to a dozen of the bigger ones, where there are also scooters, mopeds and bikes for hire.

Of course, it is not as easy as it sounds. Greek organisation and schedules leave much to be desired.

Ships

There is nowhere else in the world like Piraeus. The port of Athens for 3,000 years, it resembles a seaside bus station with ships tooting their arrivals and departures every five minutes. The quayside is lined with ticket touts, cake shops and travel agencies. The air is thick with the cries of the touts competing with the hooters of the big ships signalling their homecoming or cast-off for a distant island.

It is not a peaceful place to stay, though it can be a convenient stopover via one island ferry and another. It is always an exciting place, though you may find it hard to recapture those magic moments with Melina Mercouri in 'Never on Sunday'. There are nightclubs and prostitutes, but they are mostly clip-joints with expensive drinks and more promise than performance. And if you dive into the harbour of Piraeus today, as the carefree Miss Mercouri did, you will need a stomach-pump and a ton of detergent to remove the oil and filth of those muddy waters.

Treat the shipping schedules with healthy suspicion. Check them with notices on the spot, then double-check with other shipping offices because each ship has its own agent and even they are a bit vague about what time it goes sometimes. Even when you have double-checked, don't expect a ship to be exactly on time. They can arrive 1-2 hours late and often take half as long again to do the journey as they are meant to.

But don't imagine that you are in for a nightmare cruise wherever you go. So long as you don't expect perfect timekeeping, the ships are an ideal way to travel; cheap if you travel 'deck', which is ideal in the climate, and exciting. Every journey is an adventure, with a grandstand view of mysterious islands and hidden harbours.

Local travellers supply colour too. Black grannies may rush the ship as though their lives depend upon it. Then lie down in the hold swathed in blankets crossing themselves and huddling together with baskets, bundles of fish and even goats as though the journey could be their last. Thanks to the heat and overeating before departure, they are the first cases of seasickness if a gentle swell blows up.

There is no need to share their plight. Better to be last on board because the decks are rarely overcrowded and the turnround times are long. Then stretch out and brush up your suntan or catch up on a book. There won't be much shade, but there are always canvas chairs or wooden seats which can be transformed into a sun bed with a few towels or soft luggage.

Beware, though, of falling asleep on the deck of an island steamer in the heat of the noon sun when fresh from Britain. A friend of mine with a pale skin spent six hours stretched out on a breezy trip to Sifnos, protesting that it was not that hot. She spent her first three days on the island groaning on a bed as her kind landlady dabbed yoghurt on her scorched pink flesh to combat third degree burns.

Hydrofoils
The past few years have seen a great increase in the number of hydrofoil services operating in Greek waters. One goes from Piraeus (or nearby Zea Marina) to the islands of Aegina, Poros, Hydra and Spetse, as well as along the east coast of the Peloponnese as far down as the island of Kythera. A second main route plies the seas between Rhodes, Kos, Patmos and Samos. The Ionian islands of Zakinthos and Cephalonia have regular summer speedboat services from Patras.

It is no exaggeration to say that the advent of hydrofoils in Greece is beginning to revolutionise inter-island travel, giving quick and easy access to many more places on any one holiday.

Planes
Travelling around Greece by plane is more predictable, and the passengers more sophisticated, but it pays to book seats well in advance as the planes are small and Olympic's local offices tend to overbook local flights. There can be some pushing and shoving and an element of mystery about times, baggage and where to catch a bus to town. Even when they have seat numbers, Greeks display a competitive spirit.

That is more fun than hassle and, with a little preplanning, local flights are a fast, efficient way to travel to the islands. Most fares cost between two to three times the boat fares.

Regular travellers to Greece by night flight find the idea of flying on to an island especially appealing because most island routes are served by planes departing between 5 and 7 am. You can breakfast on your chosen island and hit the beach for a recuperative sleep between 9 and 10 am.

Athens airport can often be a snare for the unaware. It has three terminals – one for Olympic domestic flights, one for Olympic international flights and one for other international airlines. Although the actual tarmac is shared by all three, the foreign airlines' terminal is right on the other side of the runways from the Olympic terminals.

You can't walk between them and need either the interconnecting bus, which runs half-hourly during the day, or a taxi costing around 200 drachmas for the trip. So, make sure you are headed for the right terminal before you take a bus from town, and allow time for transfers between terminals.

If you do have two or three hours to kill at the airport, between an international and domestic flight, the best places to sit or sleep are the arrivals section and bar of the foreign airlines' terminal, and the departure section and bar of the Olympic international terminal. The domestic terminal very often resembles a noisy cattle-market, while the departure section of the foreign airlines' terminal is far too small and gets horribly overcrowded.

Buses
Buses are also fast and efficient for long distance trips on the mainland, and marvellously cheap, even after the latest increase in oil prices. When and where they run, they are also an excellent way of getting around islands. A bus can take 15 minutes and cost no more than 20 drachmas for a journey that might otherwise be a painful uphill toil of two hours.

But, buses do have odd hours in Greece, tending to travel at farmer's hours of dawn and early afternoon, and on some smaller

islands they simply don't exist. So it is best to be prepared to use a combination of buses, small boats, scooters, bicycles, donkeys, taxis and walking to get around.

Island transport
Caiques link many places on islands because they run around the coasts where most villages nestle and they can be hired on demand for 300-600 drachmas a round trip. Scooters are about the same (500-800 drachmas), bicycles 200-300 drachmas, and donkeys around 400 drachmas for a day hire, coming slightly cheaper by the week. Car hire is expensive and taxis usually charge around 400 drachmas for a trip of 8-10 kilometres. But sharing the cost of caiques, cars and taxis with other people does wonders for the cost per head.

Accommodation
There are a number of luxury hotels in Greece with all the facilities you would expect anywhere in the modern world – restaurants, bars, swimming pool, tennis court and 24-hour room service – and they are offered at keen prices by British package tour operators. Booked by the night, they cost upwards of 2,000 drachmas for a double room.

But, most visitors, whether on a package or travelling independently will stay in a broad mix of 1-star hotels (C, D and E category), tavernas and rooms in private houses. The cost is about 600-1,200 drachmas for a double room, rising to 1,500 drachmas in places. In my experience, the second category of accommodation is the more pleasing. Five-star hotels in Greece (Luxury, A and B category) tend to be less friendly, a lot more expensive on extras like bar drinks and wine with meals, and serve blander, less ethnic food. Because of their prices, it is doubly annoying if the plumbing doesn't work well or the tennis court is out of action because the net is missing. Such things do, alas, happen in the best-intentioned Greek enterprises.

Cheaper hotels, tavernas and private rooms are more friendly and less formal. They don't usually insist that you have breakfast, yet may serve yoghurt, honey and ice cream, however late you rise, even throwing in a cup of coffee and piece of Turkish delight on the house. You should expect a basic room with twin beds, a wardrobe, a bedside lamp and a washbasin with cold water. There may be no shade on the centre light, but often you will have a balcony with a magnificent view of the harbour, beach or wooded hillsides. If you have a small separate bathroom – and they are a growing fashion – the odds are that it will have a shower rather than bath. This will be flooded after use, but will be cleaned every day.

Renting your own villa or apartment has become increasingly popular, and most tour operators now offer a wide selection of Greek holiday 'homes'. Mainly on the big islands such as Corfu, Crete and Rhodes, these will vary greatly in both style and comfort. Hundreds of new villas have sprung up over the last few years, mostly built in that rather bland style, that now seems to be standard everywhere in the Mediterranean. But they will probably be comfortable, with some good modern equipment.

Older villas tend to have much more character. What they lack in luxury they will make up for in such attractions as a shady vine-covered patio, traditional wooden furniture and cool marble floors. A word of general warning. If tour operators brochures mention the need for car hire, they usually mean it. A daily mile or two walk for provisions under a hot August sun, can quickly dampen any enthusiasm for Greek country living.

Camping is also popular in Greece now, and if you are short of cash or plan a lot of travelling, it pays to carry a sleeping bag. There are some well organised campsites on the mainland and main tourist islands, but these are few and far between on the smaller islands. Sleeping on the beaches is not generally encouraged, but they can be used if nothing else is available, as can the deck of the ship on an overnight journey.

Eating, drinking

Some of the most memorable meals of my life, and the cheapest, have been enjoyed in Greece. Yet Greek food suffers a worse reputation than the fare of any other country in Europe.

Most Greek wine is regarded as oily or rough, while the resinated (pine-flavoured) variety is described as tasting like anything from disinfectant to turpentine. When did you read a wine writer praising Greek wine? Then people complain about the slow service, too much olive oil, cold or lukewarm food and the cost of local fish. This is all true, sometimes. But, there is another side to the story. Like so many of the best things in life, Greek food and wine requires a little effort, experimentation and patience, and improves on acquaintance.

The food is pure and healthy, free from preservatives, and close to ideal in a hot climate, once you find your way around a Greek menu and get used to the dressing. The olive oil is the best in the world, especially the dark green variety that looks as though it is fresh from the press. So are Greek olives and omelettes cooked in the oil. The tomatoes that are synonymous with salad are big and full of flavour. There are still isolated Greek island communities that have no record of a case of heart attack or bowel cancer – the two biggest killers in Western society – thanks to this kind of diet.

But there is no need to die of boredom either. If you want to break your stomach in gently on Greek food, stick to salads, omelettes, and freshly cooked fish and meat, which the oil and herbs can transform into gourmet delights at any wayside or beach taverna. The same is true of many pre-prepared dishes like keftedes (spicy meat balls), chicken, spaghetti, and moussaka. Not to mention treats like taramasalata, saziki, sofrito, gouvetsi, roast kid and suckling pig, which are not found everywhere, but are worth looking out for. So, believe it or not, are 'guts' or 'spleen', which I have eaten garnished with black pepper, raw onion and fresh basil. They are delicious.

Don't leap at the first thing offered which is invariably fish anywhere near the sea, and can be a slight rip-off. But, be prepared to try local specialities. Look for little skewers of pork kebab cooked over charcoal (souvlakia) and sliced doner kebab. Beware of lobster unless you have a long purse and sense of occasion. Greek lobster is nothing special and is rarely accompanied by the right dressing. Whereas fried squid (kalamarakia) is cheap and delicious, and so are small fish like whitebait (marides), usually cooked whole and served with lemon. In most parts of the country, they still cost around 100 drachmas a plate. Red mullet (barbounia) costs more than it should, but is usually worth the price – which should always be inquired about beforehand, as it is geared to weight. For a change try Lythrinia, swordfish, cod steaks with garlic sauce, or any fish baked in the oven with onions, tomatoes and peppers.

Fruit is often outstanding. Greek melon, grapes, wild strawberries and apricots are unbeatable. Salads are also first class and if you can't face a neat tomato salad for the seventh day on the trot, ask for it to be spiced with onion, cucumber, olives or cheese. With all of these it will become a 'Greek salad', and cost perhaps twice as much, but might make a satisfying meal without meat, fish or eggs.

If you are unhappy with Greek food, or want a light lunch, there are plenty of snack foods offering a cheap and satisfying solution. Like cheese and olives. The white goat's cheese (feta) needs olive oil to moisten it, but there are other good yellow cheeses and Greek yoghurt is creamy and full of flavour. It bears no resemblance to the insipid and oversweet fruit yoghurts sold in supermarkets in Britain. Try it with local honey or nuts. Vegetables, stuffed or served cold in olive oil, may be an acquired taste, but something to savour once you have acquired it. Especially beans and okra. Fried aubergine and marrow are another delight to look out for. In the autumn corn on the cob and chestnuts are barbecued over braziers in the street in many cities.

Treacly cakes like baclava, kadifi and galaktaboureko are good, and loukamades (sweet, spicy doughnuts deep fried) can make a meal on their own. But beware, appetising looking cream cakes are almost always synthetic and disappointing. Ice cream is a better bet, coming in cheap and varied forms with a perceptible Italian influence. Cake shops often sell chilled rice puddings, custards and cream caramels that make a perfect finish to a savoury meal in a restaurant, which may not offer any sweet courses or may be restricted to one seasonal fruit.

Have you ever tried wild capers? These prickly shrubs are often pickled on the islands and served up for variety with tomato salads, giving them an unusual flavour. They can also be boiled and, prepared that way, kept many islanders alive during the deprivations of the Second World War.

Greek wine ranks, for my money, in the middle of the second division. It cannot stand beside the sophisticated wines of France, Spain and Italy, but what it lacks in depth it makes up in variety.

Pride of place goes to retsina, the golden yellow wine laced with pine essence, handed down from Ancient Greeks and maybe even from the Gods themselves. The pine gives it a distinctive flavour and acts as an amazing preservative. Retsina defies the idea of a wine that 'won't travel' and is so cheap – around 40p a bottle at the last count – that it defies belief. It may taste like disinfectant, turpentine or mouthwash to the uninitiated, but to me it tastes like nectar. I am an unashamed fan. It is the first thing I would take to a desert island if I had a refrigerator. Properly chilled, it is the perfect complement to Greek food on a hot day, apres swim at lunchtime, or with dinner on a warm evening. It comes in 500 grm bottles which are enough to make two people feel at one with the world and one to feel transported. Two bottles can take you into paradise.

Now I savour my retsinas. I know all the foibles of the Attic retsinas – Plaka (a trifle chemical), Kourtaki (sharp, but friendly), Deka Ephta or 'Seventeenth' (thin, but cooling), Kamba (costly, but sophisticated) and Pikermi (near to perfect when well-chilled). Retsinas from other areas include Vinko of Kos, CAIR of Rhodes, Kechri and Malamanda of Salonica, Achaia Klaus and Patraiki from Patras. On the smaller islands, retsina often gets matured in barrels and served in tin decanters. Rough, but just as delicious as its bottled counterpart, it can be seen as the Greek equivalent to farmhouse scrumpy.

Besides retsina there are many other good local wines. On Rhodes, white Lindos and Rodos compete for favour with the dry red Chevalier du Rhodes. The elegant sweet and dry wines of Samos will stand beside the best wines of the world. The flinty white Rombola and red Manzavino of Cephalonia are worth tracking down. The smokey whites and reds of Santorini taste perfect on the spot, as do the fruity brown wines of the western Cyclades, Kythnos, Seriphos and Sifnos. Paros has its own distinctive red Naoussa wine, usually served cold. Athens, Salonica and the Peloponnese have large ranges of sophisticated wines going under brand names like Santa Laura, Mount Hymettus, Boutari and Kamba. Demestica from Patras is found almost everywhere in Greece and is dependable and moderately priced. I find the red a trifle brackish, but the white is refreshing, mild and flavourful.

If service is a problem in a Greek restaurant – and it often can be – try asking for a bottle of wine as you walk in. It can work like a charm in capturing a waiter.

Always pick up a menu on the way in if there is none on the table, or, if it is clearly that kind of place, walk straight towards the kitchen to see for yourself and order from the cook. This is the custom in many places, especially in northern Greece, where they often display the day's specialities in trays under a heated glass cabinet. But beware ordering wine so enthusiastically that you attract the attention of local winos. I once had to spend every evening on Skyros making small talk in my limited Greek with a local priest who was world champion retsina drinker. He had been exiled from Athens

to that isle of drinkers and the locals swore he drank 24 bottles a day.

Zitsa, in Epirus, offers the nearest thing to Greek champagne, a sparkling fruity wine often corked in small beer sized bottles and sometimes in gold topped champagne sized bottles.

The beers are often welcome in high summer, but they tend to be frothy and chemical. Horrible when warm. They would not pass the CAMRA test. But, Greek mineral waters are superb, while chocolate milk in cartons is also good chilled.

Ouzo, the ubiquitous aniseed spirit that turns white in water, is a drink to be taken sparingly. So is Greek brandy, which varies in taste from 2-star petrol to Armagnac. It can exact a five star vengeance if overdone. A friend and I neatly polished off a bottle after dinner after two bottles of wine in Lindos one cool week in December. Afterwards we went to walk off the meal and had to crawl back on hands and knees to find our rented villa. The next morning was spent in a darkened room praying to Bacchus to melt away the steel bands tightening around our heads.

Don't judge eating places too harshly by their appearance. A lonely beachside hut run by a sleepy fisherman can turn out the best red mullet or pork chops you have ever tasted. One of my most memorable lunches on a recent visit to Greece was served up by the twin cafes at Ioaninna bus station in half an hour between the Igoumenitsa express arriving and the sleek air conditioned Salonica express departing. Two juicy kebabs, two cool glasses of wine, bread, cake and Nescafe were served on demand at a total cost of 50 drachmas, all with a welcoming smile. Compare that reception and fare with the soggy sandwiches and tea of an English bus station.

Greek coffee is served everywhere at every hour and is a solemn ritual. It is tastier than the imported 'Nescafe', though sometimes too small for satisfaction. Try a 'diplo' (double) and 'metrios' (half-sweet).

15

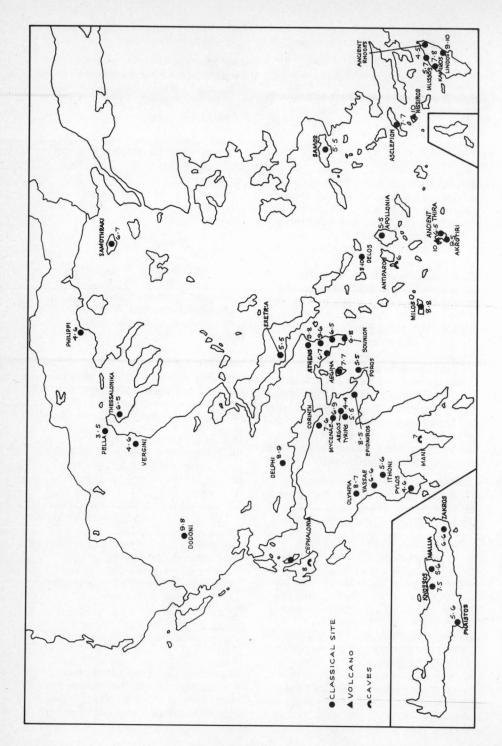

ANCIENT RHODES

4·5

MILOS 5·7 KAMIROS 7·8

LINDOS 9·10

NISSIROS

IO 7·7

ASCLEPION

SAMOS 5·5

SAMOTHRAKI 6·7

APOLLONIA 5·5

ANCIENT AKG·S THIRA

PHILIPPI 4·6

DELOS

ANTIPAROS

SIKINOS

IO 6·9 AKROTIRI 9·5

MILOS 8·8

THESSALONIKA 6·5

ERETRIA 5·5

8·8 9·6 6·5

SOUNION

ATHENS 6·7

6·8

PELLA 3·5

VERGINI 4·6

AEGINA 7·7

5·5

PAROS

CORINTH

MYCENAE 7·6

ARGOS 6·9

TYRINS 5·4

5·5

EPIDAVROS 8·5

DELPHI 8·9

MANI 7

OLYMPIA 8·7

VASSAE 6·6

ITHONI 5·6

PYLOS 4·6

DODONI 8·9

CEPHALONIA

8

KNOSSOS 7·5

MALLIA 5·6

ZAKROS 6·6

PHAISTOS 5·6

● CLASSICAL SITE

▲ VOLCANO

◖ CAVES

16

Which Site Guide

Greece is the striking point of the anvil of the ancient civilisation that stretched from Egypt to Mesopotamia. It has been at the cross roads of history ever since, and is endowed with historic and religious remains of a variety and quality given to few countries.

If Herodotus were alive today, he would be hard pushed to select only seven surviving Wonders of the Ancient World in Greece. Take Delos, Santorini, Mycenae, Delphi, Olympia, the Athenian acropolis, the Lindos acropolis, the Asclepion on Kos, Knossos, the amphitheatres of Epidavros and Dodoni, and the aquaduct and temple of Hera on Samos. They're a dozen to start with. And these are well matched by a collection of spectacular medieval or Byzantine sites in Mount Athos, Meteora, Patmos, Monemvasia, the turreted villages of the Mani, Mystras, the old towns of Rhodes and Kos, Naufplion, Dafni, Ossios Loukas and the Khozoviotissa monastery on Amorgos.

Most of the best sites are on the mainland or Peloponnese, which do not always make the best beach holiday territory. True also of two of Greece's outstanding museums – those of Athens and Thessalonika.

The temples in Athens are well preserved despite the ravages of the Turks, who used the Parthenon successively as a brothel and gunpowder magazine during their occupation, and the British archaeologists like Elgin, who took the best bits of sculpture for the British Museum. But the Athenian acropolis and the surrounding Theseion, Forum, Temple of Zeus and Hadrian's gate lack something in atmosphere, surrounded as they are by the dust and heat of a busy city and the constant blaring of horns and squeal of tyres.

Thessalonika suffers the same fate. Its ancient city walls, the Arch of Galerius, his tomb and the old city baths are fringed by building sites and busy roads.

Most of the sites of old battles and scenes from mythology like Marathon, Themopolae, Salamis, Mounts Olympus and Ida have nothing left to show for their place in history other than atmosphere.

If you have a keen taste for history, the best place to savour the ancient world is the Peloponnese, which boasts the citadel and beehive tombs of Mycenae, the amphitheatre of Epidavros, Olympia, Nestor's palace at Pylos, Tiryns, and the old cities of Argos, Corinth and Sparta. Climb the citadel of Mycenae at first light when there are no other tourists around and take a long look down the Argive plain towards Naufplion, where Agamemnon must have landed on his return from Troy. The Peloponnese gives easy access across the Gulf of Corinth to Delphi, scene of many similar crucial events. There are the smouldering ruins of the Mani, the Byzantine city of Mystras, the old town of Monemvasia and the castles of Methoni, Argos, Naufplion and Mystras.

Northern Greece is the nearest rival to the Peloponnese. It boasts Philippi – scene of two battles which decided the fate of the Roman Empire when Anthony defeated Caesar's murderers. Pella was the birthplace of Alexander the Great, and Vergina is believed to be the last resting place of Philip of Macedonia. Both are within easy reach of Thessalonika. If these sites are a trifle disappointing beside their Peloponnese rivals, the same cannot be said about the monasteries of Meteora and Mount Athos, which stand comparison with anything of their kind in the world.

But you can take to Homer's wine dark sea

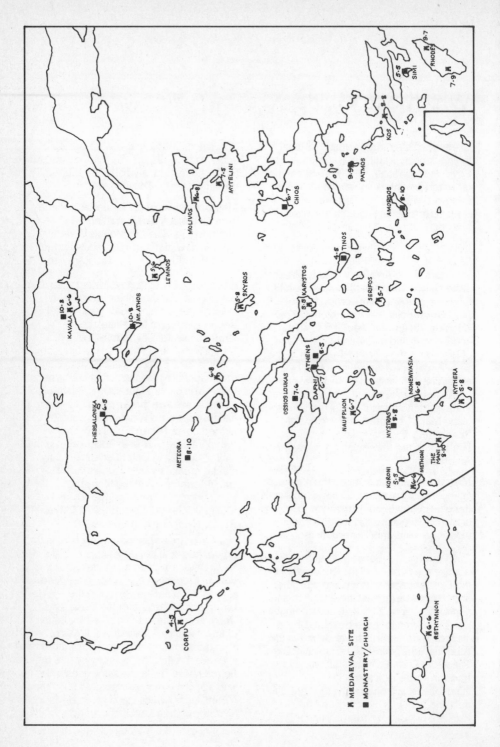

RHODES 9·7

SIMI
7·9

KOS 8·8

PATMOS 9·9

AMORGOS 8·10

MYTELINI 7·5

MOLIVOS 6·8

CHIOS 6·7

TINOS 4·5

LEMNOS 5·6

Mt. ATHOS 10·9

KAVALA 10·8
6·6

SKYROS 5·8

KARYSTOS 5·5

SERIFOS 5·7

MONEMVASIA 6·8

KYTHERA 5·8

ATHENS 5·5

DAPHNI 6·7

OSSIOS LOUKAS 7·6

NAUPPLION 6·7

MYSTRAS 5·8

THE MANI 8·10

METHONI 6·5

KORONI 5·5

THESSALONIKA 6·5

METEORA 8·10

CORFU 4·5

RETHYMNON 6·6

✗ MEDIAEVAL SITE
■ MONASTERY/CHURCH

and sail in the wake of the heroes on a cruise around the Greek islands, taking in both sites and beaches on the way. Almost every island has some remains from the distant past.

Follow wily Odysseus on his way around the Ionian Isles. Set off from Corfu where he was washed ashore on the long voyage from Troy. Wander down to his home island of Ithaca, which has a few relics of prehistory that may or may not belong to the hero, and call on the way at Cephalonia, whose cave is the nearest thing to the Styx I have seen. It is not a great archaeological tour, but good for conjuring up the past.

Or take the route of Jason and the Argonauts across the north Aegean to Lemnos, Thassos, Samothraki, Chios and Lesbos, bearing in mind that if you want to press on to the golden fleece country, you may have to enter Turkey via Chios or Samos. Chios and Samothraki have their share of ancient temples and Chios, Lemnos and Lesbos all have well preserved castles.

Theseus spent most of his time in Athens, but he also spent time on Naxos, Skyros and Crete, if the legends are to be believed. Naxos has ancient statues carved from the rock, Skyros the ruins of a castle and monastery, and you can now visit the labyrinth of Knossos on Crete without getting lost or tangling with the minotaur. It is also possible to call on the way at Santorini (where the famous eruption ended the Minoan rule) and see more local classical sites, plus the emerging Minoan city of Akrotiri.

The Greek heroes who sailed to besiege Troy also sailed across the North Aegean from Aulis around Evia and via Lesbos to the mainland. Again there are some interesting sites to see on the way, though you have to take one of the authorised trips to Turkey to see the site of the seven cities.

You could see more, though, by plotting your own archaeological journey across the central Aegean via Mykonos, Amorgos, Samos and Patmos to Kos and Rhodes. Delos is a satellite isle of Mykonos, and it and the other five islands share between them the most impressive sites in the Aegean – ancient and mediaeval. Rhodes has the acropolis of Lindos as well as three early Greek towns, while Patmos boasts the most splendid monastery on the islands.

One Greek hero, Perseus, had a novel way of travelling in those days. Instead of putting up with the rigours of sea travel, he strapped on a pair of golden sandals and flew to other islands from his home in Serifos. Icarus tried the same trick with wax wings, but came to grief when he flew too near the sun and was deposited in a pool of wax on Ikaria. Those who find sea travel a problem can perform this ancient trick with a flight schedule from Olympic Airways as most of the big archaeological sites are linked to Athens by air.

SITES TO BUILD A JOURNEY ON

Webster rating (max 10 marks)	BUILDINGS	SETTING
CLASSICAL		
Athens and the mainland		
Athens:		
Acropolis	9	8
Theseion	9	6
Temple of Zeus	6	5
Aeropagus/Pnyx	3	6
Sounion	6	8
Thessalonika:		
Tomb and Arch of Galerius	6	5
Roman walls, baths and		
market	6	5
Delphi	8	9
Philippi	4	6
Vergina	4	6
Pella	3	5
Dodoni	9	8
Peloponnese		
Corinth	7	6
Mycenae	6	9
Epidavros	8	5
Pylos	4	6
Vassae	6	6
Olympia	8	7

	BUILDINGS	SETTING
Ithomi	5	6
Tiryns	5	5
Argos	4	4
Evia		
Eretria	5	5
Cyclades		
Delos	8	10
Milos: catacombs	8	8
Naxos: Apollonia	5	5
Santorini:		
Akrotiri	9	5
Ancient Thira	6	5
North-east Aegean		
Samos	5	5
Samothraki	6	7
Crete	7	5
Knossos	5	6
Mallia	5	6
Phaistos	6	6
Zakros		
Rhodes	9	10
Lindos	7	8
Kamiros	5	7
Ialissos	4	5
Ancient Rhodes		
Dodecanese	7	7
Kos: Asclepion		
Saronic islands	7	7
Aegina	5	5
Poros		
Ionian islands	4	6
Ithaca		

MEDIEVAL

Athens and the mainland

	BUILDINGS	SETTING
Athens: churches	8	5
Dafni	6	7
Meteora	8	10
Mount Athos	10	8
Ossios Loukas	7	6
Thessalonika: churches	6	5
Kavala	6	6

Peloponnese

	BUILDINGS	SETTING
Mystras	8	8

	BUILDINGS	SETTING
Monemvasia	6	8
Argos	5	6
Naufplion	6	7
The Mani	8	10
Methoni	6	6
Koroni	5	5
Evia		
Karystos	5	5
Dodecanese		
Patmos	9	9
Kos	8	8
Simi	5	5
Rhodes		
Castle and old town	9	7
West coast castles	7	9
Crete		
Rethymnon	6	6
Cyclades		
Amorgos	8	10
Serifos	5	7
Tinos	4	5
Sporades		
Skiathos	6	8
Skyros	5	8
North-east Aegean		
Lemnos	5	6
Lesbos:		
Molivos	6	8
Mytileni	7	5
Chios	6	7
Ionian		
Corfu	4	5
Kythera	5	8

NATURAL WONDERS

	BUILDINGS	SETTING
Peloponnese		
Mani caves		7
Cyclades		
Santorini: volcano		10
Antiparos: cave		6
Ionian		
Cephalonia: caves		8
Dodecanese		
Nissiros: volcano		10

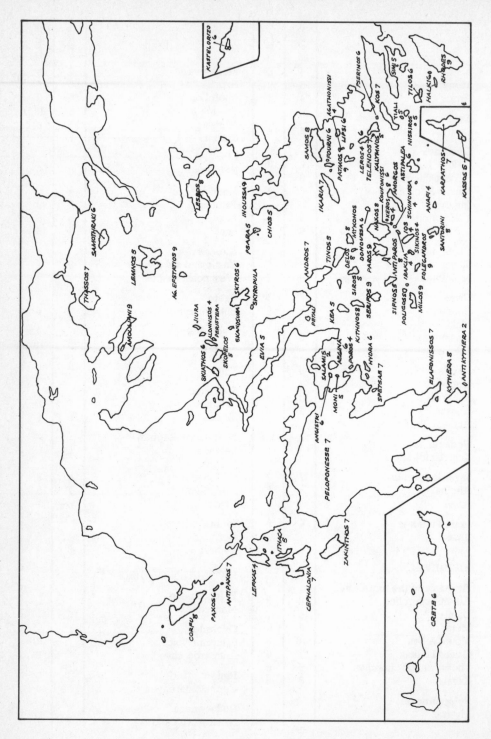

Which Island Guide

Odysseus, Jason, Theseus and the other heroes had the right idea. They sailed their ships over wine-dark seas, spurning the elements and inertia of their countrymen, to visit the beautiful islands of the Ionian and Aegean seas. Each had a quest and each was seeking his own idea of paradise and perfection.

Modern travellers to Greece can follow in the wake of the heroes and seek out the perfect Greek island. Probably they will never find it, but they will always find something special on the way.

By using the Which Island Guide you can pick out at a glance the right island for your Greek holiday this year. The 80 islands listed have been put into four groups:

Tourist Isles
Lesser Tourist Isles
Quiet Isles
Remote Isles

They all have star ratings for accessibility, scenery, eating out and sites. All these plus Trevor Webster's personal rating for their beaches and overall appeal as a perfect Greek island.

Islands with Webster rating of 9 marks

Agios Efstratios
Amouliani
Folegandros
Inoussa
Milos
Paros
Patmos
Rhodes
Serifos

KEY

Accessibility
**** international airport with direct flights from Britain
*** quick and easy travel on from Athens (by air or sea) or other Greek airport
** journeys from 4-9 hours from Athens and other Greek airports
* irregular ferry services and/or long ferry journeys

Scenery
**** spectacular
*** special
** pretty
* average

Eating out
**** excellent variety of food and choice of restaurants
*** above-average food
** average
* limited choice and/or few restaurants
o none, or extremely little food available

Sites
**** spectacular
*** several interesting sites to see
** one or two sites
* limited
o no sites at all, or none that are worth visiting

Special features
‡ recommended for families
△ volcano
© caves

General island rating:

9	7&8	5&6	4 and under

Which island guide
TOURIST ISLES

Webster rating
(max 10 marks)

	ACCESSIBILITY	SCENERY	EATING OUT	SITES	SPECIAL FEATURES	SAND BEACHES	PEBBLE BEACHES	OVERALL ISLAND APPEAL
Aegina	***	**	***	*	‡‡	4	5	6
Corfu	****	****	****	*	‡‡	9	8	8
Crete	****	***	***	***		4	8	6
Delos	* **	***	○	****		0	0	8
Evia	***	***	**	*		5	6	5
Hydra	***	***	***	○		0	4	6
Ios	**	***	**	○		4	1	4
Kos	****	***	***	***	‡	6	6	7
Mykonos	****	***	****	○		9	2	8
Naxos	**	***	**	*		4	5	8
Paros	***	***	****	*	‡	9	2	9
Peloponnese	***	**	**	****		5	6	7
Poros	***	**	**	*		1	2	4
Rhodes	****	***	****	****	‡	9	8	9
Samos	****	***	**	**		6	6	8
Santorini	****	****	**	***	‡ △	5	4	8
Sifnos	**	***	**	**		4	2	5
Siros	**	**	***	○		6	2	5
Skiathos	****	***	****	*	‡	6	6	6
Spetse	***	**	***	○	‡‡	4	5	7

Which island guide
LESSER TOURIST ISLES

Webster rating (max 10 marks)

	ACCESSIBILITY	SCENERY	EATING OUT	SITES	SPECIAL FEATURES	SAND BEACHES	PEBBLE BEACHES	OVERALL ISLAND APPEAL
Alonissos	**	**	*	O		1	6	4
Andros	***	**	***	O	‡	6	2	7
Antiparos	**	***	***	*	‡©	8	2	8
Chios	***	**	**	*		3	5	5
Ithaca	**	**	**	*		3	4	5
Kalymnos	**	**	*	O		4	2	5
Karpathos	***	***	**	O		6	5	7
Kea	***	**	**	O	‡	3	2	5
Cephalonia	****	***	**	*	‡©	3	4	7
Lemnos	***	**	***	O		4	2	5
Lesbos	****	**	**	*		4	5	8
Milos	***	**	**	*		8	4	9
Patmos	**	***	***	**	‡	6	6	9
Paxos	**	**	**	O	‡	2	4	6
Salamis	***	*	*	O		2	2	2
Skopelos	**	**	**	O		2	5	5
Skyros	**	***	**	*	‡	6	2	6
Thassos	***	**	***	O	‡	6	6	7
Tinos	**	**	*	*		3	2	5
Zakinthos	****	***	***	*	‡	6	2	7

Webster rating
(max 10 marks)

	ACCESSIBILITY	SCENERY	EATING OUT	SITES	SPECIAL FEATURES	SAND BEACHES	PEBBLE BEACHES	OVERALL ISLAND APPEAL
Amorgos	★★	★★★★	★★	★		5	4	8
Anafi	★	★★	★	○		2	2	4
Angistri	★★	★★	★★	○		3	2	6
Astipalea	★	★★	★	○		2	2	6
Folegandros	★★	★★★	★★★	○		4	4	9
Halki	★	★★	★★	○		4	2	6
Ikaria	★★	★★	★	○		5	5	7
Kassos	★★	★★	★★	○		1	5	5
Kimolos	★★	★★	★★	○		8	2	8
Kithnos	★★	★★★	★★	○		6	2	8
Kythera	★★★	★★★	★★	★		5	2	8
Lefkas	★★	★★	★	○		1	5	4
Leros	★★	★★	★	○		1	5	4
Moni	★	★★	★★	○		2	2	5
Nissiros	★★	★★★	★★	★★	△	2	4	5
Samothraki	★★	★★	★	★		3	2	6
Serifos	★★	★★★	★★	★		5	2	9
Sikinos	★★	★★	★	○		2	2	4
Simi	★★	★★	★★	★		1	3	5
Tilos	★★	★★	★★	○		4	4	6

Which island guide
REMOTE ISLES

Webster rating
(max 10 marks)

	ACCESSIBILITY	SCENERY	EATING OUT	SITES	SPECIAL FEATURES	SAND BEACHES	PEBBLE BEACHES	OVERALL ISLAND APPEAL
Agathonissi	*	*	*	○		2	2	4
Amouliani	*	**	*	○		3	2	9
Antikythera	*	*	○	○		2	2	2
Antipaxos	*	*	○	○		3	2	7
Agios Efstratios	**	**	**	○		6	2	9
Donoussa	*	*	*	○		4	2	6
Elafonissos	**	*	*	○		3	2	7
Fourni	*	**	**	○		4	2	6
Inoussa	*	**	**	○		6	2	9
Iraklia	*	*	*	○		2	2	4
Kastelorizo	*	**	*	○		3	2	6
Keros	*	*	*	○		2	2	4
Koufonissi	*	*	*	○		2	2	6
Lipsi	*	*	*	○		2	2	6
Poliegos	*	*	*	○		3	2	5
Psara	*	*	**	○		2	2	5
Pserimos	*	*	*	○		3	2	6
Schinoussa	*	*	*	○		2	2	4
Telendos	**	**	*	○		3	2	7
Yiali	*	*	*	○		3	2	5

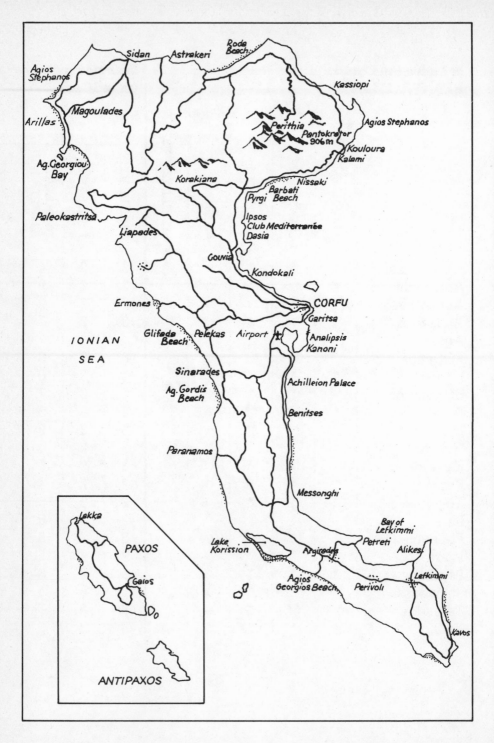

Agios Stephanos
Sidan
Astrakeri
Roda Beach
Kassiopi
Arillas
Magoulades
Perithia
Pantokrator 906m
Agios Stephanos
Ag.Georgiou Bay
Korakiana
Kouloura
Kalami
Nissaki
Paleokastritsa
Barbati Beach
Pyrgi
Liapades
Ipsos
Club Mediterranée
Dasia
Gouvia
Kondokali
CORFU
Garitsa
IONIAN SEA
Ermones
Glifada Beach
Pelekas
Airport
Analipsis
Kanoni
Sinarades
Achilleion Palace
Ag.Gordis Beach
Benitses
Paranamos
Messonghi
Bay of Lefkimmi
Petreti
Lake Korission
Argirades
Alikes
Agios Georgios Beach
Perivoli
Lefkimmi
Kavos

Lakka
PAXOS
Gaios
ANTIPAXOS

28

The Big Five

Corfu, Crete, Rhodes, Evia and the Peloponnese are the Big Five islands in tourist terms.

It may be denied that the Peloponnese is an island and even Evia is often treated as part of the mainland, while Crete has been called the sixth continent. Corfu and Rhodes, for their part, fit neatly into the Ionian and Dodecanese groupings, but deserve more detailed treatment than their sister isles.

What the Big Five have in common is easy access by ship and plane and good road networks that facilitate exploration of their most remote corners and beaches. They all have powerful histories and more relics of bygone civilisations than most Greek isles.

Corfu

Corfu, or Kerkira, is green, gentle and slightly British. You don't see it immediately in the peeling grandeur of the tall buildings in Corfu town, which are Venetian with two castles to match. But cricket is played occasionally on a brown ground speckled with green, flanking the main public square, and you can drink ginger beer at the cafes that line the Rue de Rivoli arcade opposite.

Many Corfiot children speak good English and you cannot pass a school playground without a flock of blue frocked girls flying to the railings to chorus 'Hello' and 'Goodbye'. Two popular bars in the harbour are 'Dirty Dick's' and 'The Spoty Dog' (and they know about the spelling). The island saw a brief British occupation in the 19th Century and today sees more summer visitors from Britain than any other Greek isle. It has other connections, being the birthplace of Prince Philip and the playground of the literary Durrell family.

Familiarity has bred contempt in many Grecophiles, who say the island 'is not really Greek'. Is it because Corfu doesn't have the sun-baked appearance of most Aegean isles and is so green and fertile that it looks as though it is rained upon every other day? In fact, from May to October it rarely rains on the island, and this happy combination of long hot summers and a luxuriant vegetation makes Corfu the nearest thing to a modern Garden of Eden that Greece has to offer. It abounds with flowers and sweet scents and terraces of grapes and tomatoes are flanked by rows of cypress trees and groves of old twisted olive trees. No wonder Odysseus was persuaded to tarry in the kingdom of the Phaecians on his long voyage from Troy, Shakespeare chose it as the setting for The Tempest, and Napoleon said his biggest regret was the loss of Corfu to the French empire.

Corfu town sports a faded elegance that is matched by few other towns in Greece. It has a Venetian castle, a peeling grey relic of a governor's palace – now turned into a museum, the Mon Repos palace, where Prince Philip was born, and the Church of Agios Spyridon, the island's patron saint, after whom every third Corfiot boy seems to be named. The streets are narrow and the houses tall. Washing lines are often stretched across from one building to another and the stuttering tones of motor bikes echo through the alleyways, while pigeons, gulls and swifts wheel overhead. Flocks of little birds give a spectacular aerobatic display over the main square nightly when the road is closed to traffic and a mass walking (the volta) takes place. It is a pleasant town to walk in. Even on the main roads the biggest risk to pedestrians seems to come from horse-drawn landaus with a multi-coloured fringe on top and jangling bells. It is also a good town to eat in, with pasta dishes imported across the Adriatic and local stews adding variety to the normal Greek diet.

Corfu is one of the most accessible isles in Greece, thanks to the overnight ferry route from the heel of Italy and a modern airport set on one of the island's lagoons five minutes from the town. It is also an easy island to explore, thanks to a web of roads, regular buses and a mass of hire shops with scooters, bicycles, mopeds and cars.

You can swim almost anywhere south of the town, but the water is cloudy along the long promenade around Garitsa Bay, so it pays to walk the 2 kilometres to 'Mon Repos' beach or take the road out of town. The main road south runs close to the east coast, which is sheltered by the mainland of Epirus and so usually has calm waters. But swimming is often off rocks or pebble beaches until you reach the deep south around Messonghi and Kavos. Down there is some perfect sand.

Just out of town the road runs across the end of the airport runway, where only a rusty traffic light separates the unwary from the slipstream of a jumbo jet. It then passes close to Corfu's most famous landmark, the tiny Pontikonissi, or mouse island, with its 13th Century chapel. Just past here you are within 2 kilometres of the Achilleion Palace, built by the sad Empress Elizabeth of Austria and featuring a statue of Achilles wounded in his heel, but still happily holding his spear. The palace has been described as ugly, but it stands in a superb setting high over the coast surrounded by cypresses and artistic gardens. Today it is the most beautiful casino in Greece and if you don't fancy trying your luck at the surprisingly costly tables, stroll down to the circular restaurant below the palace which has a superb view of the town far below and a resident hoopoe, who chimes out his strange call every five seconds or so through the evening. Or go and look at the remains of the curious Kaiser's Bridge down on the coast.

This is the main villa coast of Corfu, and English travel company signs stretch down to Benitses and beyond where big hotels now compete with humble tavernas for the custom of foreign holidaymakers.

Beyond Messonghi, the road leaves the coast and passes through pretty inland villages with houses painted green, pink, blue and brown in a fashion typical of Corfu. It then runs through the narrowest part of the island where there are beaches to choose from to the left and right. Near the Korission lagoon, these include the long sandy Agios Georgios, which shares its name with another long sandy strand on the north-west of the island, and yet a third fanning out from Roda on the north coast. Kavos on the southern tip was just two houses and a donkey when I first went there in the sixties. Now it is a thriving resort with hotels and restaurants, visited by regular boatloads of day trippers from hotels up the coast, attracted by its long sandy beach. There is no problem getting away from the trippers in this part of the island. There are sand spits everywhere. Follow one of the many signs to small coves, or walk along Kavos or Agios Georgios beach until there is no-one else in sight.

The west coast of Corfu is similarly abounding in beautiful sandy beaches, a feast for anyone with a small boat or yacht. The easiest to reach from town are at the resorts of Glyfada, Agios Gordis, Ermones and Mirtiotissa.

Ermones is not a great beach, but is within walking distance of the clubhouse of the Corfu Golf Club, from which some superb olive greens stretch down the Ropa valley. You can do 18 holes before lunch and swim in the afternoon in the bay where the naked Odysseus was supposedly washed up before Nausicaa and her handmaidens on his long trip from Troy. Green fees are modest and you can buy a reasonable week's golfing package, including transport from Glyfada.

Paleokastritsa, with its hills, sandy bays and the 13th Century Angelocastro, could easily be the site of the Palace of the Phaecians. Today it is a busy resort connected to Corfu town by a smooth motorway and best known for the lobsters kept in wooden cages in the bay and served in the restaurants. If you snorkel in the bay and take a look at the poor imprisoned creatures in the water, you will probably settle for red mullet and save a small fortune on your bill. The best view of Paleokastritsa is from the road that winds from the resort to Lakones and Makrades; there is another great view of the coast from the pretty village of Pelekas crowned by the Kaiser's seat.

Go a little further afield and you can find less crowded beaches. Try Paramones, reached through 'the black forest' of Agios Kontogialos, just south of Glyfada. Or Agios Georgios, reached either through Pagi village or via Afion. It is one of the most spectacular long sandy beaches in Greece and was hardly visited by tourists ten years ago. Nowadays there are three good tavernas, regular boat trips around the headland from Paleokastritsa, and approach roads that are one up on third class river beds.

A tarmac coast road to the north-west of the island has transformed that area into a holiday coast with activity centering on the little resorts of Agios Stefanos and Arillas, both with reasonable beaches. The north coast has the older resort of Sidari, with its sandy bay and strange rock formations.

Further east is Roda, on another of the island's long sandy beaches. Here a new resort with smart long-stay apartments called Anaharavi is growing up on the same bay.

Kassiopi, on the north-east corner of Corfu, is another place that time has transformed. Ten years ago it was a small fishing village. Now it abounds with hotels, restaurants and discotheques. There are good beaches nearby and it gives the best view over the narrow straits to mysterious smouldering Albania. You can see the lights of a small village twinkling across the water at night, but cross at your peril. If there are any tourists there with binoculars they must have provoking thoughts about this island where so many people romp about in bikinis on mopeds and water-skis while they tour wire factories and collective farms.

The north-east coast was the setting of Lawrence Durrell's 'Prospero's Cell' and Gerald Durrell's 'My Family and Other Animals'. Every cove contains a small fishing hamlet with a sheltered pebble beach and a romantic name like Koloura, Kalami, Kentroma or Agios Stefanos.

Closer to Corfu town is the long white pebble beach of Nissaki and the long sandy strands of Dassia and Ipsos. This is the place where the Club Mediterranee built a holiday village of thatched huts many years ago and they have now bought two small hotels. It is a boisterous area and the Club's noisy boat outings can shatter the peace of any small cove to the north.

Kondokali is another holiday village which has grown out of recognition over the past ten years. Sandwiched between a sandy beach and limpid lagoon, it is now a bustling place, widely featured on many package tour programmes.

Corfu has little to offer in the way of archaeology and this may explain the recent creation of 'The Village' – a place you mustn't leave Corfu without visiting, if you obey one of the thousand signs dotted around the island. For about £4 including drink, you can see a recreated Greek village with all the old-style handicrafts done before your very eyes. In the bars and tavernas a three course dinner comes dear at 600 drachmas; so do drinks. However, I must admit I enjoyed my evening visit to 'The Village', but it is an odd idea on an island abounding in so many natural pretty villages.

I was more struck by an eerie little ghost village called Perithia on the cool north slope of Pantocrator that I struggled up to one morning. There, far from the madding crowd, you can get a glimpse of what village life over the past 300 years must have been like, disturbed only by the occasional bark of a dog or a curious glance from a member of the two families who still live there. Most of the inhabitants have moved to another village closer to the coast and you are not surprised when you

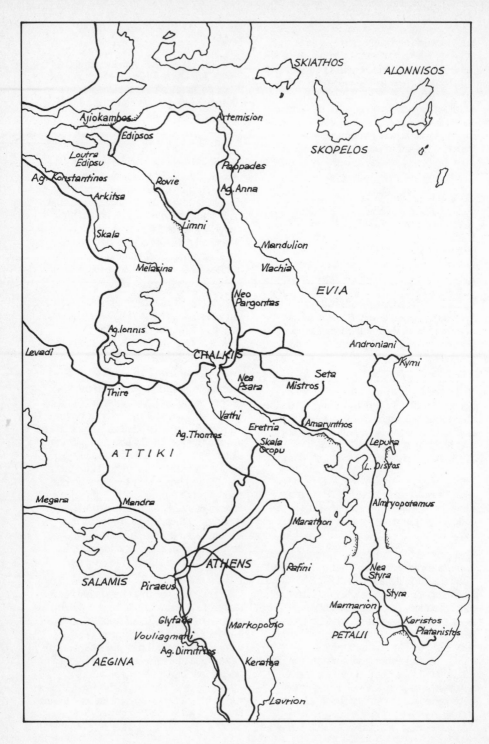

CORFU

Away from the coastal
resorts, Corfu is still
surprisingly rustic.

CRETE

The plateau of Lass...
of the biggest vegeta...
in Greece.

ne
dens

RHODES

Rhodes' superb Old Town is one
of the best memorials to the
Crusades.

see the state of the road that winds up to Perithia. Yet it repays a painful journey by foot or scooter and boasts a small bar to refresh the weary traveller though you may feel that you have to waken the dead to get a drink.

Travel

FLIGHTS
International scheduled and charter flights.
Up to 6 flights daily from Athens (55 mins).

BOAT
Up to 8 crossings daily from Igoumenitsa (1 hr 55 mins). There are 4 buses daily from Athens, Kifissou Street terminal, to Igoumenitsa (9 hrs 30 mins). Ferries also from Patras and daily ferries from Brindisi in Italy (8 hrs). Corfu is also on numerous cruise ship routes.

Evia

Greece's second largest island is, incredibly, hardly known outside the country. A shame really for, with good sandy beaches, easy access from Athens and some magnificent scenery, Evia (or Euboea) lacks little for the average holidaymaker. Admittedly it does not have an ancient civilisation of its own to show, or pretty whitewashed harbours, and sometimes feels like an extension of the mainland, but many people who catch a glimpse of the coastline en route for Andros and the Sporades are pleasantly surprised.

Evia stretches like a man in a sack along the eastern coast of Attica. The contours fit exactly with the mainland, just as though the island has drifted away some time in the past. It does seem probable that Evia was torn away from the mainland by an earthquake. Writers of the Classical period speak of tremors and volcanic activity in the region, and both green marble and lignite are mined in the interior, indicating an unusual geology.

Now the Gulf of Evrikos is narrow in places and the island and the mainland almost

touch at Chalkis, where they are joined by a swing bridge. The channel has been challenging Evia's status as an island, since the early 5th Century BC.

This makes Chalkis a natural gateway to Evia – though there are easy ferry crossings via Glifa, Arkitsa, Oropos, Aghia Marina and Rafina. Chalkis is a bustling port, lined with restaurants serving a variety of seafood and amazing quantities of ouzo on summer evenings. There is an additional bustle every time the tide turns and a convoy of ships and fishing smacks move through the narrow straits.

North of Chalkis the three main seaside resorts are Limni, Gregolimano and Aedipsos. Limni has a harbour, beach and monasteries nearby, Gregolimano has the best sandy beach, and Aedipsos has the most distinguished mineral springs in this part of the world. Modern sufferers with rheumatism can take the same thermal waters patronised by Roman emperors like Augustus, Nero and Hadrian.

Take the road around the north coast of Evia via Pefki, Vassilika and Kimassi and you will find the island's best beaches, wide open stretches of sand a short walk away on the left side of the road. Kimassi also has occasional trips by caique to the nearby islands of Skiathos and Skopelos.

The middle section of the island is split by high wooded mountains ranging up to 5,800 feet, which make the east coast steep and inaccessible except at Kimi where a high mountain village is linked by a good serpentine road to a beach resort of the same name. Kimi is an honest, rather than pretty, harbour with a long jetty for ships to Skyros, and a serviceable sandy beach.

Eretria and Karystos are the big seaside resorts in southern Evia. Eretria is the closest rival to Chalkis in size and has a regular short ferry crossing from Skala Oropos on the mainland. It also boasts tombs, baths and an ancient theatre with an underground passage from the wings to the centre stage through which the demon kings of old made their dramatic entries. There are organised beaches along the coast to beyond Amarinthos, another small village with a ferry service to Oropos. Nea Stira, Marmari and Karystos all offer good swimming in the south of Evia, as well as ferry connections with Rafina. Karystos has the best sandy beach and a well preserved Venetian fortress nearby.

Evia has a good road network and regular buses connect all the main towns and villages.

Travel

ROAD	Buses from Athens, Liossion Street Terminal, every 30 minutes. (1 hr 50 mins).
BOAT	Daily crossings from Rafina to Karystos, Marmari and Nea Stira; from Skala Oropou to Eretria and from Arkitsa to Loutra Aedipsos in the north of the island. No crossing takes longer than 2 hours. Evia also has ferry connections from Kimi on the east of the island to the Sporades and north-east Aegean islands.

Crete

Crete is where mythology and history met around 1500 BC. The meeting place was the Labyrinth of Knossos, known in legends as the lair of the dreadful Minotaur, a half-man, half-bull monster who enjoyed an annual sacrifice of young Athenian boys and girls, until meeting his comeuppance from Theseus. Around the turn of this century, a labyrinth was discovered at Knossos by the British archaeologist Sir Arthur Evans, and the myth entered the pages of history. But such evidence as there is suggests the labyrinth was only a ceremonial place, and the young Athenians were trained as acrobats to take part in the dangerous bull dances as portrayed on the walls of Knossos.

There are modern myths about Crete too. It is often described as the most Greek of Greek islands, with picturesque towns, superb beaches and wild scenery and people. The facts only fit half of this picture.

The Cretans can look wild and woolly in their village dress with knife stuck in baggy trousers, tucked in long boots. The mountains are grand and awesome in places, but Crete is no undeveloped wilderness.

Although the biggest Greek island (discounting the Peloponnese), it is heavily populated with fertile valleys and some sprawling, ugly towns. Multi-storey hotels along the north coast lend a strong commercial streak to the hordes of tourists who flock there annually, and some of the wilder beaches and caves of the south coast are inhabited by hordes of students and the 80's equivalent of hippies all summer. The island is also intensively cultivated. Crete is reckoned to produce ninety per cent of the Greek currant crop, an eighth of its wine and a quarter of its olive oil. Its hills are also covered with strips of tobacco plants.

There are a number of long sweeping sandy beaches, notably along the north coast at Aghios Nikolaos, palm-fringed Vai, Malia, Rethymnon, to the east of Heraklion and to the west of Chania. But, for its size, Crete does not have good beaches. The south coast is mainly rock and pebble, the good north coast beaches are crowded and one strand near Heraklion is the only pay beach I have encountered away from the Athenian Riviera.

However, Crete is often the first island people visit in Greece and many people speak well of it after seeing other islands. It is clearly one that evokes strong feelings, and undoubtedly has great colour and character. Crete is the land of the lotus-eaters, the home of 'Zorba the Greek', and the main centre of the Minoan civilisation. It has only joined Greece in earnest in the past fifty years; before that it had a separate history and fierce independence that was revived during the Second World War. Then, Crete fought long and bravely against the German occupation and stories of the resistance abound to this day. In the hill villages away from the coastal tourist strip, men with long moustaches, scars and stained cartridge belts that appear to have been worn for

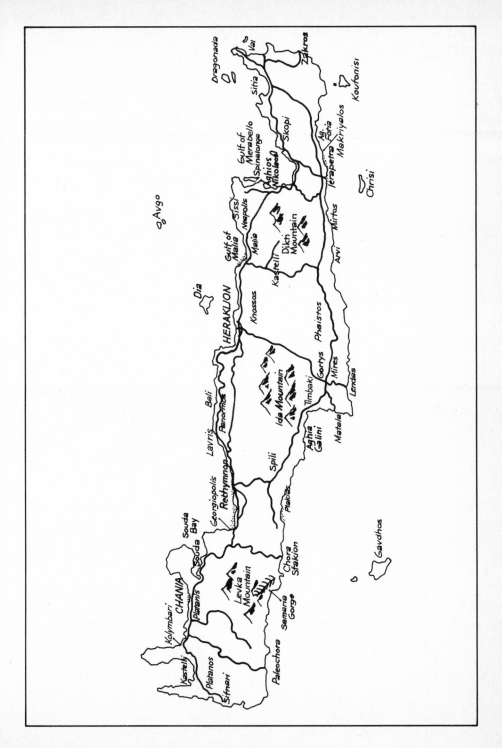

forty years, with full sound effects will proudly reconstruct battles they fought as partisans in the early 1940's.

No island can more rightly claim to be the cradle of European civilisation. When the Minoans ruled Crete, and perhaps most of the eastern Mediterranean 3,500 years ago, they lived in richly-frescoed palaces with ingenious drainage and lavish entertainment. Their women wore make-up, jewellery and fashion clothes, and unashamedly bared their breasts. You can see it all portrayed on the walls at Knossos, the most famous Minoan site built around 1700 BC. Knossos has to be seen by anyone interested in archaeology, art, or just plain humanity, but it is a shame that it stands on the edge of a dusty suburb of Heraklion and I feel that Evans went overboard in his bid for popularisation. The fresh black and red paint on the columns and the brown-painted concrete slabs that serve as wooden beams stand side by side with crumbling stones, the world's oldest flush toilet and tall terracotta vases. It is somehow reminiscent of an abandoned film set.

Although it is only just emerging from the dust, the Minoan city on Santorini puts Knossos in the shade for my money, and the unreconstructed remains at Malia on the north coast of Crete and Phaistos in the south give better ideas of the proud settings of Minoan cities. All may yet be eclipsed by the palace still being excavated at Zakros on the east coast of Crete, which is a little off the beaten track, but mercifully has been pillaged only by time.

The capital of Heraklion shares with Knossos the look of a partially reconstructed ruin, due to some unfortunate wartime bombing and poor rebuilding. As the main port of Crete with the airport along the coast, it is the natural gateway to the island, and boasts good cheap restaurants, but should be abandoned after a look at Knossos, a visit to the splendid archaeological museum and a meal at one of the town's many satisfying restaurants. Fortunately, Heraklion boasts a good bus service and there are scooters

for hire; cars too, but they cost a Minoan ransom.

Sad to say, Chania, the island's administrative centre, is almost as ugly and downbeat as Heraklion, despite a colourful facade. It sometimes teems with sailors from the nearby naval base at Souda Bay. Chania and Heraklion are not everyone's favourite towns.

There is far more character in the second division of towns on the north coast; Rethymnon with its castle, minarets, narrow streets, houses with wooden bays and balconies, and one of the best sandy beaches in Crete; Malia with a long golden beach and small island to swim out to; Sitia, the major town of eastern Crete with a grey sand beach nearby; Georgiopoulis on a sand beach between Rethymnon and Chania; and Aghios Nikolaos.

Aghios Nikolaos was a natural choice for the setting of the TV serial 'The Lotus Eaters', as it is now for many British package tour firms. A pretty town, it teems with bars and restaurants along the quayside and inner harbour. There are sandy beaches within walking distance, and these are protected by the bay from the strong waves that often pound the north coast of Crete. Aghios Nikolaos also has its quota of lively discotheques, motor bike hire shops and a good bus service. Elounda, 10 kilometres away overlooking Spinalonga island, also has beaches within walking distance.

Modern lotus-eaters often make for the south coast, where a greyish sand that is unique to this part of Crete combines with pebble beaches. But, the seas are calmer and the warm breezes that drift across from Africa make the coast a pleasant place to linger even in January and February. It helps to explain why Ierapetra, with its long beach, and cave strewn Matala further west, became such favourites for campers, students and hippies in the 1960's. Nowadays they are rivalled by Paleochora – with its long curve of sand, Sfakia, Aghia Gallini, Matala, Peramata and Aghia Fotia as holiday centres. Three of the best sand beaches along this south coast are at Makrys Gialos, Plakias and Arvi. None of these villages have particularly attractive harbours by the standards of smaller islands, although Aghia Gallini with its busy waterfront disco scene and string of shingle coves, is drawing a growing number of British package tours these days.

There are always pretty villages inland and Crete has good connections by buses that run along the first class road network that connects Heraklion with the whole of the north coast, and selected areas of the south. There are also scooters and mopeds for hire in many towns and villages.

Travelling inland in Crete it is hard not to miss a series of spectacular gorges, of which the most famous is the Gorge of Samaria, claimed as the largest in Europe. You can comfortably walk its 18 kilometres of Castle Dracula scenery – towering peaks and rushing springs and waterfalls – in a day, but have to make provision for the return journey and allow four or five hours for the walk. Fortunately, motor boats run along the coast (1½ hours) from the exit of the gorge at Aghia Roumeli to Chora Sfakion, which has a fair bus service with a connection to Chania and other south coast villages early in the evening. And, if you get lost in the gorge – which is hard to do because the stony paths are well marked – you won't be alone. Even in winter you meet people walking down Samaria.

Another memorable sight of inland Crete is a dance session staged for a wedding or festival. You might see war dances, the cyclical Syrtos and the romantic Sousta performed by men and women in national dress, employing flute, lyra, mandolin and even bagpipes for lively, wailing melodies.

Walking enthusiasts, or mule riding fans, staying in Aghios Nikolaos can cross the plateau of Lassithi with its hundreds of windmills irrigating one of the biggest vegetable gardens in Greece, and climb Mount Dikti. Near the village of Psychro is the deep cave of Diktaion where legend says Zeus was born and hidden from his father Kronos, who had a strange yen to eat his new born son. It has a grotto rich in

stalagmites and a resident phantom, according to imaginative visitors.

Another place to hunt phantoms is the islet of Spinalonga, a few miles off the coast from Aghios Nikolaos or Elounda. It used to be a leper colony and is now a deserted old village, with creepy creaks and bangs breaking the silence when the wind is blowing.

Minoan Crete ended with a bang around 1500 BC when volcanic Santorini blew its top in the biggest eruption in recorded history, but the island has more recent remains at Gortys, south of Heraklion and north of Phaistos. This was the seat of the Roman Governor of the island and you can see the outline of his residence, a temple of nymphs and other sanctuaries dating from the 2nd Century AD.

Ships go from western Crete to Antikythera and the Peloponnese, while ships from Rhodes, Kassos and Karpathos call at Aghios Nikolaos and Sitia. Ships for Piraeus sometimes go from Souda Bay as an alternative to Heraklion.

Travel

FLIGHTS International charter flights to Heraklion and Chania.
From Athens:
Up to 7 flights daily to Heraklion (45 mins).
Up to 4 flights daily to Chania (45 mins).
Up to 2 flights daily to Rethymnon (via Chania) (45 mins).

BOAT Direct daily sailings from Piraeus to Heraklion and Chania. Aghios Nikolaos, Sitia and Heraklion are also on ferry routes for boats to and from Rhodes, Karpathos and central Cyclades islands. Crete is also on many cruise ship routes.

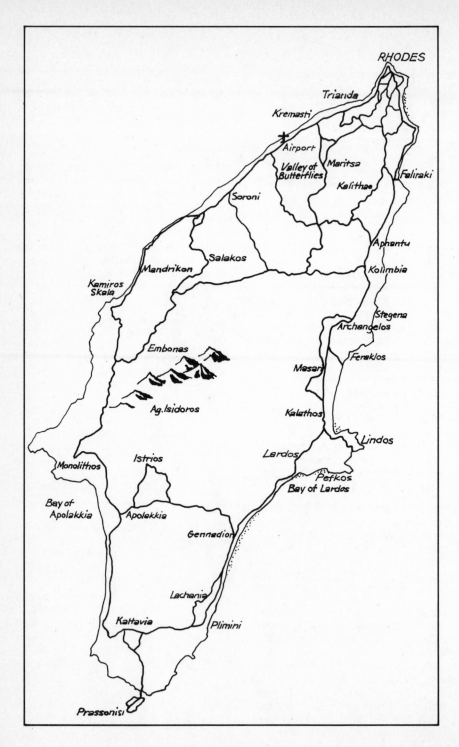

RHODES
Trianda
Kremasti
Airport
Valley of Butterflies
Maritsa
Kalithae
Faliraki
Soroni
Aphantu
Mandrikon
Salakos
Kolimbia
Kamiros Skala
Stegena
Archangelos
Embonas
Feraklos
Masari
Ag.Isidoros
Kalathos
Lindos
Istrios
Lardos
Monolithos
Pefkos
Bay of Lardos
Bay of Apolakkia
Apolakkia
Gennadion
Lachania
Kattavia
Plimini
Prassonisi

Rhodes

Two towns in one, a beautiful coastline, a remarkably green interior and the most breathtaking acropolis in Greece are the crowning glories of Rhodes. And, that's just the start.

Although not the most southerly isle of Greece, it often has the best yearly climate, with less rain than mountainous Crete, winds from the south in winter and the temperature rarely falling below 50°F. An appropriate setting for the valley of the butterflies and countless hot weather blossoms like bougainvillea, oleander, hibiscus and rhododendrons. You can swim in the sea here without discomfort up to December, although you may have to dry quickly and take a couple of sweaters for the cool evenings.

Situated 250 miles south-east of Athens and 10 miles off Turkey, Rhodes new town is the most modern and loveliest in Greece, albeit somewhat un-Greek. Its broad tree-lined avenues, smooth harbour and arched public buildings are legacies of the Italian occupation which lasted up to 1943.

The old town is fresh from the Crusades and one of the best memorials to those bloody plundering expeditions masquerading as holy wars. The medieval walls, the neatly walled harbour, the Castle of the Knights, their hospital and the Palace of the Grand Master, look at first sight like an imaginative film set. In fact the high walls were used in 'The Guns of Navarone' and more recently in the TV series 'The Dark Side of the Sun'.

It is hard to believe that the Street of the Knights dates from the 14th Century; it is so perfect. Only the glass and crowds of camera-hung tourists spoil the illusion. What a shame there is no trace left of the Colossus that bestrode Mandraki harbour in ancient times and stood proudly among the Seven Wonders of the World, until toppled by an earthquake in 225 BC.

Dining out in the old town is a lovely experience, with lights reflecting from the cobbles and the old walls, though there are many good restaurants in the new town competing for your favours with a wide variety of Greek dishes laced with a number of international ones. For nightlife there are cinemas and theatres and a hundred bars and discos competing for custom. There's also a casino at the Grand Hotel, where all you need is a smart suit, your passport and a supply of ready money.

The Palace of the Grand Masters is used nightly for sound and light displays in summer and there is almost a permanent wine festival in the Rodini Park on the outskirts of town. With a wide variety of CAIR wines (Compagnie Agricole et Industrielle de Rhodes) on tap, and swans floating on ornamental ponds, Rodini makes a good setting for this festival of Dionysos.

Rhodes town has good sandy beaches on both sides of the promontory, but they can be crowded and expensive for those who want to rent umbrellas and eat close by. Fortunately, they stretch almost uninterrupted – along with big hotels – for three or four kilometres on the north side of the island. From then on the beaches run almost continuously along both shores, with the best natural strips of sand stretching for miles at the far end of the island. Like many other islands in Greece, there is a rough side and a calm side. There almost always seem to be pounding waves on the exposed northern shore, while they are rare on the south coast.

Most visitors who leave Rhodes town to tour the island, especially those who have arrived by cruise ship, head for the Valley of the Butterflies, the three ancient cities of Rodos, Ialissos and Kamiros and the acropolis of Lindos.

The Valley of the Butterflies, or Petaloudes, is near the island's international airport on the north coast. A diversion from the coast road leads to a green valley of streams and waterfalls where thousands of orange moths cling to mossy rocks, feed on the resin of storax trees, and fill the air at the sound of footsteps or clapped hands. They are a summer seasonal phenomenon, though, and revert to plain grubs in winter.

Ancient Rodos is within walking distance of town, on the oddly-named Monte Smith, where a stadium and two temples overlook the suburb of Rodini. Ialissos is sited on a high hill a few kilometres off the airport road and has a pretty monastery as well as the remains of temples set in avenues of cypress trees. However, the two most impressive sites are further from the town, at Kamiros on the north coast and Lindos, 55 kilometres along the southern shore.

Kamiros has retained the complete layout of a 3rd Century BC city with temple, market and streets full of houses. Not only that, but it is in a glade of pine trees set high above the shore.

Lindos is one of the jewels of Greece. Now an exceptionally popular holiday resort, it is a dazzling white town of winding streets laid with pebbles, built on a high promontory above two bays – sandy Lindos Bay and the almost enclosed rocky Bay of St Paul where the Apostle is supposed to have landed. As if that were not enough, the hill rises into a cliff, on top of which is a castle surrounding a magnificent acropolis of 4th and 5th Century temples perched high above the blue sea. If the ruins don't match those of the acropolis in Athens, the setting makes up for it. View it, though, at 9 am before the coaches and donkeys arrive.

The cliff face of Lindos was used to house the big guns in 'The Guns of Navarone', and the film kept the donkey drivers of Lindos happily employed for weeks carrying equipment up the steep steps to the acropolis. Usually, their main traffic is tourists, as the village itself is kept free of traffic.

It is small wonder that coaches by the dozen stream down the road from Rhodes to Lindos. The pity is that most of their passengers see little else of the island, which has a fresh delight around every headland. On the eastern side the road south from Rhodes town hits the coast first at the long sandy beach resort of Faliraki, busy with a strip of restaurants and package hotels. Then come a succession of quiet strands, reached by road or track;

Afantou with its pearly green golf course nearby; Tsambika with its rocks; Kolimbia with its two sandy bays and rooms, restaurants and windsurfing and where the sea floods into a smooth sandstone crater; Stegena with its harbour; and Haraki, where a pretty fishing village is overlooked by Feraklos castle and the skeletal remains of Typaldos villas, started when the cruise line was at its zenith in the mid-sixties, then abandoned like a modern monument.

Beyond Lindos to the south, the coast road runs by one continuous beach, interrupted here and there with shapely rocks, all the way down to Plimmiri, a beautiful curving bay complete with restaurant beneath an abandoned Italian village. Then the ring road around the island turns inland for Katavia and Agios Pavlos, a curiously abandoned group of Italianate buildings set in a plain of cornfields and cypress trees. From there the intrepid can take a poor track down to the southern tip of the island at Cape Praso Nisi, with its two long strips of sand, nearly a mile long and among the best beaches on Rhodes.

Beyond Katavia the asphalt road peters out, but the beaches get better. The sandy dunes flanked by the coast road on the south-west coast of Rhodes along Apolakia Bay stand comparison with any beach in Greece but the sea tends to be on the rough side. The amazing thing is that this area is almost deserted, even in high summer. It seems to be penetrated only by a few who rent scooters in Rhodes town (at 800 drachmas a day) and the occasional air-conditioned coach doing a swift spin around the island without stopping. Alas for many, fortunate for a few, only a handful of the island's bright orange service buses go south of Lindos. Those that do go at the crack of dawn or late in the evening. Also there is little accommodation in the deep south, though there are welcoming restaurants and rooms at Genardi, Plimmiri, Katavia, Lardos, Kiotani and Apolakia.

The road along the north coast then moves inland to the villages of Siana, Monolithos and Critinia, passing two Castles of the Knights on the way. Off the main road near Siana a new beach resort is emerging at Glyfada, but, the beaches are pebble. The castle of Monolithos is most spectacular, perched on a peak and surrounded by a gorge. Skala Kamiros is an attractive little fishing harbour with rooms and restaurants and an average beach that has daily boats to Halki in summer. The beach improves again around Kamiros itself and there is good swimming all the way along to Rhodes town, provided the sea is not too rough.

The inland villages of Rhodes have their own particular charm and it is worth pausing a while, en route for Lindos, in ones like Archangelos. A white town of the plain but now bypassed by the road, it lives up to its holy name. But leave plenty of time for trips inland across the island in the south and stick to the roads actually marked on the only good map available (published by Clyde Surveys). The roads are poor and wind through thick pinewoods. The signposts are worse. I have spent several cool winter evenings trying to find my way back to Lindos on a scooter taking a road across the island that promised a short cut of only a few kilometres, but has turned into a long day's journey into night. It is easier by far to take a day trip along the coast by the regular caiques and yachts that run from Mandraki harbour. These also provide the sea links with Simi, Halki and Turkey. For longer trips to Kos, Patmos and Samos, the new hydrofoil service has cut the ferry times by nearly two-thirds.

Travel

FLIGHTS	International charter flights. Up to 4 flights daily from Athens (55 mins). Daily summer flights to Kos, Santorini and Karpathos.
BOAT	Daily sailings from Piraeus via Cyclades or Dodecanese islands (20 hrs). Rhodes has good ferry connections to all nearby islands and is also on many cruise and scheduled routes from other countries.
HYDROFOIL	Summer service to Kos, Patmos and Samos.

The Peloponnese

The isle of Pelops is a man-made island cut off from the mainland by the narrow, steep-sided Corinth Canal, completed less than a hundred years ago. It links the Saronic Gulf to the Gulf of Corinth and saves ships bound for Athens from the west, the best part of a day trip around the four spurs of the Peloponnese, including the notorious Capes of Matapan and Maleas, dreaded by sailors since the siege of Troy.

But the Peloponnese has always had some of the characteristics of an island, separate from the Greek mainland. Thanks to the narrow and easily defended isthmus of Corinth, it gave birth to a series of proud city states in the Ancient World, including Corinth, Sparta, Mycenae and Argos, which all in their turn successfully challenged Athens for supremacy and spawned their own civilisations.

This moody, myth-strewn land is bigger than Crete and encompasses far more fascinating historical remains than that island and Athens put together. The mood is most evident in the Mani, Olympia and Arcadia, where the hills seem to echo strange sounds and you expect to find Pan playing his pipes around every corner. The myths and the history are strongest in the Argolis peninsula, where four strong city states were once founded and the first capital of modern Greece was established by the youthful King Otto at Naufplion in 1833.

The gateway to the Peloponnese is Corinth, a pleasant modern town with an esplanade and seaside gardens, but far outshone by the glories of Ancient Corinth a few kilometres away. Here there is the massive Doric temple of Apollo, dating from the 6th Century BC, the old market buildings and the newly excavated port of Lechaion, all sited below the Frankish-Venetian castle on Acro Corinth.

Another 45 kilometres by bus – of which there are plenty in this part of the world – lies Mycenae, one of the most awe-inspiring sites of the Ancient World. There,

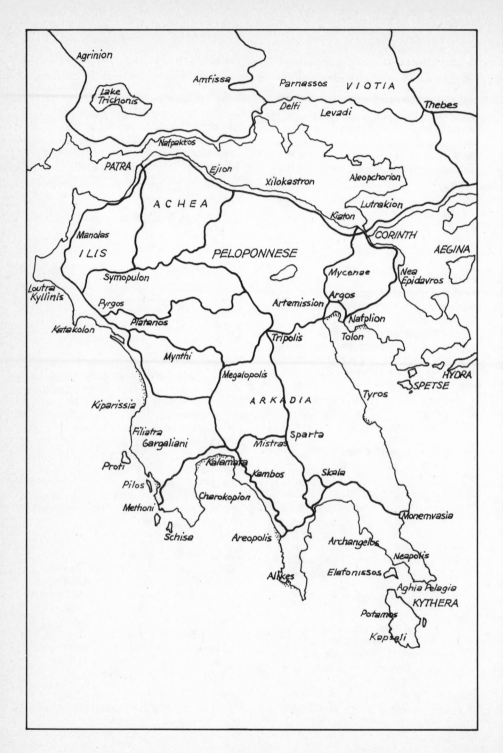

the German archaeologist Henrich Schliemann sprang a revelation on the world in 1882 by opening a beehive tomb containing the golden mask of Agamemnon. The mask is now in the Archaeological Museum in Athens, but the tomb of Agamemnon and that of his disloyal wife Clytemnestra, are there in Mycenae on the left of the road that leads up to the citadel.

The atmosphere of the citadel is magic. Entered by the Lion Gate, it lies on a low hill, backed by higher ones looking down the full length of the Argive plain to the other ancient cities. As you stand in the throne room of this royal palace, it is easy to conjure up the ghosts of Agamemnon and other heroes of the Trojan War.

After that the next two cities of the plain, Nemea and Tiryns, come as a slight anticlimax since they do not have the height or the remains of Mycenae and Argos. But Tiryns has its fans who see images of a different kind in the walls of big stones in which Hercules was supposed to have been born.

Twelve kilometres down the plain, lies Argos, which gave its name to the entire peninsula of the Peloponnese. Modern Argos is a busy, dusty town with one of the most frantic bus stations I have encountered in Greece. But, a healthy climb from the town brings you to the summit of a hill where there is an impressive Frankish castle with the remains of the old city – theatre, market place and Roman baths – at the foot.

From there it is but a short step to Naufplion, a dramatic town with a Venetian fortress set on a high rocky headland, from which the houses spread down to the sea on both sides. It has dozens of hotels and restaurants, regular buses from Athens, and a passable pebble beach, which all go to persuade many people to make it their centre for a sight-seeing tour of Argolis. My preference would be one of the seaside resorts of the peninsula like remote Kataklion or Korphos. Also Nea Kios or Tolon, which both have good sandy beaches and a more relaxed atmosphere.

Tolon is a popular British summer resort with a good dune beach to the north of the village and boats running to two offshore islets for those who find the village beach too crowded.

Another alternative is the pretty port of Epidavros. Now easily accessible, thanks to the road developments of recent years, it is only a few kilometres from the green grove that houses the best preserved ancient theatre in Greece. Drama is still performed here at Epidavros during a festival that runs through July and the early weeks of August.

If you want a more extended rest at the seaside after toiling around ancient sites in the heat of summer, take the road south to Porto Heli or Costa at the tip of the Argolis peninsula where you can find good sand on the beaches and regular boats to the islands of Spetse and Hydra, and a swift hydrofoil to Athens.

Ships and express buses proceed down the east coast to Tyros, Plaka, Leonidion, Kyparissi, Geraka, Monemvasia and Neapolis, all on the eastern trident at the base of the Peloponnese. Pass by the others, but don't miss Monemvasia, which is the Mont St Michel of Greece. It is a high, almost sheer rock rising out of the sea, joined to the land by a narrow causeway, on which is a gaunt Byzantine town with churches, mansions and castle. You can stay on the landward side of the connecting spit and swim from a beach that stretches away to the north, though some prefer to swim from the rock. But the best place to eat is in the town. Follow the lights down the winding streets for a choice of good restaurants in the evening.

Neapolis is a straightforward coastal town, but it has a fair beach and easy sea connections for Elafonissos and Kythera. Further up the coast there are some quiet sandy beaches at Plytra and Elia.

The middle spur of the trident is altogether more dramatic. The road through Tripolis, in green Arcadia, winds down first to Sparta and then to the area known as the Mani. Strangely, there is little left of Ancient Sparta – an odd, but perhaps

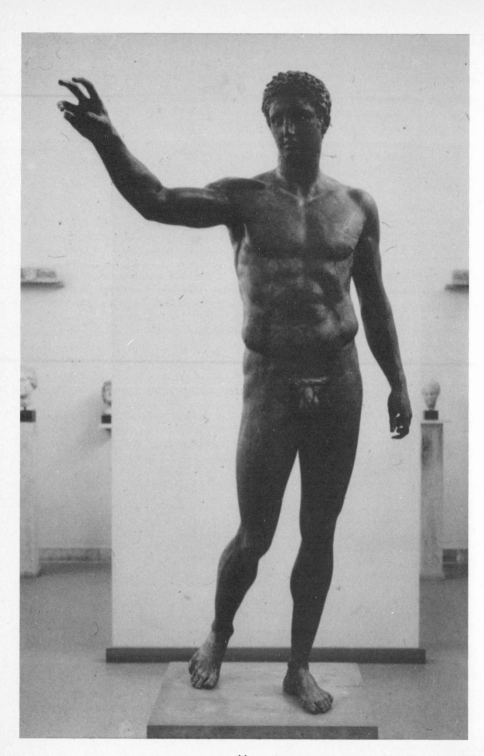

fitting, memoriam to that stern military dictatorship – but above the modern city of Sparta ranges the dead Byzantine city of Mystras, another of the historical wonders of Greece. On the crest of the hill stands the ruined fortress built by the Frankish prince William Villehardouin in 1249. He did not last long, but his Byzantine successors continued his work building palaces and churches at Mystras. They are beautiful buildings in an appropriate setting and contain some pretty frescoes.

If Monemvasia and Mystras fail to conjure up some ghosts from the past, then the Mani should do the trick. Unique in the whole of Greece is this haunting region of turreted villages set in wild mountainous scenery. Stretching from the colourful ports of Gythion and Areopolis in the north to Gerolimin in the south, the villages of the Mani are largely deserted. But their souls live on in the stone watchtowers rising above almost every house, said to be what the warring Maniot clans built up during the night in order to pelt their enemies with stones during the day. It is hard to say that these are pretty towns and villages, but they have the fascination of a Dracula film. As you wander through narrow streets, overgrown with cacti, twisted olives and prickly pear and overshadowed by tall towers, the bark of a dog or the braying of a donkey echoing through a village can be a little spine-chilling.

The National Tourist Organisation are bravely preserving Vathis as a traditional settlement. They are converting it into guesthouses but, in doing so, possibly may have lost the unusual nature of the place. It has stood uninhabited for centuries on a promontory with its towers rising amid natural crags overlooking the sea.

This is not a great area for swimming, since the beaches in places like Gythion and Gerolimin tend to be stony, but it is one for boating, through the caves of Pyrgos Dirou with their strange forests of stalactites and stalagmites.

There are a few isolated inviting beaches on the road north of Areopolis. Kalamata at the head of the Messinian Gulf has long stretches of beach, but the town itself is one to be passed through quickly, along with others in the Peloponnese like Pyrgos and Tripolis. They are noisy, chaotic and sprawling, and there are better places to linger. Three of these down the western spur of the Peloponnesian trident are Koroni, Methoni and Pylos. Pylos, with the palace of Nestor and the Bay of Navarino, is where Telemachus came to seek word of his father Odysseus from wise old Nestor, and it is also where the fleets of Britain, Russia and France combined in the cause of Greek Independence and sank a fleet of Turkish galleys in 1827. It is possible to take a boat from Pylos to visit Nestor's cave and the war memorials to the dead of the three allies. Also to take a swim in a sandy bay and search on the way back for skeletons of Turkish ships, which can be seen under the sea on a calm day close to the islet of Sfakteria at the head of the bay.

But you must make sure you know the exact price for the trip you plan before you go. The wily boatmen of Pylos, like those of the Styx, are apt to raise the price at every stage of the journey. Nestor's palace lies 20 kilometres north of Pylos and some claim that it is the best layout of all the surviving Mycenaean palaces. It certainly must have been one of the cleanest if you can judge from the clay bath tub and jug that stand there still.

The road runs north from Pylos through pretty Kyparissia, which has a good sand beach, to some of the best beaches in the Peloponnese. After the hot spa resort of Kaiafa, set on an island in a lake, they come one after the other; Katakolo, Skafidia, Kourouta, Kyllini and Kolagria. I would choose Kyllini, which has fine, golden sand and dunes around a modest little resort and is another spa with mineral springs. It also has quick boat connections to the beautiful islands of Zakinthos and Cephalonia.

Before Kyllini the road forks right at Pyrgos for Olympia, another of the amazing collection of antiquities in the Peloponnese. The sacred grove of the original Olympic Games in a lush green valley with springs, conveys something of the spirit of the early gatherings. The site is largely a layout of columns, which give a clear picture of the buildings as they were.

You can still run around the arenas where athletes gathered every four years from 776 BC to 393 AD. The Games stopped only when a Christian emperor of Rome committed a most unchristian act and ordered the sanctuary to be destroyed. Fortunately, his lackeys did not do their work too well.

An inland route from Kalamata to Olympia offers more feasts for archaeology students who are not crazy about sandy beaches. They can take in five sites on the way, including the amphitheatre of Ithomi in a grand green setting of hills and cypress trees, and the Doric temple at Vassae, a twin of the Parthenon in Athens and one of the best preserved in the Peloponnese.

Patras, standing at the point of entry to the Gulf of Corinth, is the first city many people see in Greece if they travel by ship from Italy or motor down the coast of Western Greece and take the ferry crossing at Rion. It is the third biggest city in Greece and somehow more friendly and negotiable than Athens and Thessalonika. It is the home of fine wines, brandies and ouzos.

Patras has good sea connections to the Ionian isles, rail and road connections (along a national highway) to Athens, and convenient buses to nearby beach resorts like Kaminia, Psathorpirgos and Lambiri, where sand leads down from pine woods. I would always travel along the north coast of the Peloponnese by bus (four hours to Athens) rather than train, as I find it hard to forget a painful, albeit friendly, eight hour journey from Patras to Corinth in the early sixties.

The north coast has other beach resorts like Aigion, Xilocastro, Seliantika and Kiato for those who want to avoid staying in big towns like Patras and Corinth. There is a ferry crossing to Itea across the Gulf for easy transfer to Delphi, a site that rivals the best of the incredible number the Peloponnese has to offer.

Travel

FLIGHTS	Flight daily from Athens to Kalamata (40 mins).
TRAINS	Daily trains from Athens to Corinth, Argos, Tripolis, Kalamata, Pyrgos and Patras.
ROAD	Frequent buses from Athens (Kifissou Street Terminal) to all parts of Peloponnese.
BOAT	Ferries from Athens serve the Eastern Peloponnese; from Patras to the Western Peloponnese. There are also fast hydrofoils (especially during summer months) from Zea marina (near Piraeus).

Ionian Islands

A chain of seven green islands, known in Greek as the 'Eptanisa', straggles down the west coast of Greece and halfway around the Peloponnese. They are called the Ionian isles after the sea between Greece and Italy, and have a common history that dates back to the days of Odysseus. Their history has been extended by successive occupations by the Venetians, the French and even the British, who ruled the islands as a 'protectorate' through the middle years of the last century.

They are all fertile, floral isles and are prone to earthquakes, like the one that wrecked many villages on Cephalonia and Zakinthos in 1953. Here you see red tiled or even corrugated roofs and high buildings rather than the whitewashed squat cubist style of the Aegean.

Kythera is the odd island out; barer, southerly and served by ships that run down the east coast of the Peloponnese and the Saronic Gulf. But, there is never any easy logic to Greek island groupings.

Corfu, Paxos, Lefkas, Cephalonia and Ithaca are linked by island steamers. Lefkas can also be reached by a road causeway. Zakinthos, Cephalonia and Kythera are served by regular ferry services from the Peloponnese coast, as well as being on the domestic air routes.

Paxos

Three hours sailing time south of Corfu town, lies the little island of Paxos, a fairly quiet place, especially after the hustle and bustle of its more famous neighbour. Tourist and local development has been limited by a shortage of water on the island.

Gaios port is almost like a miniaturised town with houses, restaurants and pensions, plus a former British residency, clustering around one main square. You can rent a room by the harbour and see the funnels of the island steamers in close-up travelling past your balcony window.

The island is so small that it is not hard to walk to find a private swimming place on any part of the coast, but most are rock or shingle. The east coast has high cliffs above the caves at Stakhai and coves at Ermitis.

An easy bus ride from the port takes you to the sandy bay of Lakka in the north by a road that passes through lush olive groves and close to the pretty harbour of Longos.

If you have exhausted all this, there are then boat trips to the sandy beach of Kavos on the southern tip of Corfu, over to Parga with its three sandy bays on the Epirot coast opposite, and around the island to the sea caves where, they say, you can sometimes see seals at play. I must have made the trip in the wrong season for the seals, but can vouch for plenty of other sea life on the way. There are regular island steamers from Paxos to Fiskardo and Sami on Cephalonia, and on to Ithaca. Caiques carry keen beach fans to the satellite island of Antipaxos.

Antipaxos

Antipaxos is barely inhabited and visited only by yachts and beachcombers from Paxos, but it has two superb beaches, including Voutoumi, which boasts a fine pale sand. It takes about half an hour by boat from the quay at Gaios.

Travel

BOAT	Daily ferry from Corfu (3 hrs). 3 ferries a week during summer months from Patras (9 hrs). Daily caique to Parga on mainland.

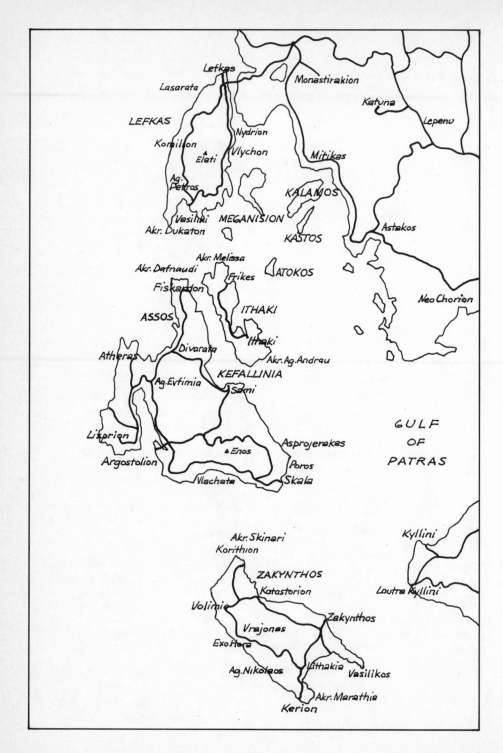

Lefkas

Lefkas is only just an island. A strip of land overlaid with a good tarmac road stretches across the limpid lagoons that surround the main port and links it with the mainland. On the way over you pass a tall castle, flat-bottomed fishing boats and seagulls resting on the piers of an old Turkish aquaduct.

All this gives the town a character that is lacking in its buildings, despite their timber-framed Turkish style. They have never been properly repaired since the last big Lefkas earthquake in 1948 and they make Lefkas the shanty town of the Ionian Sea. Stay elsewhere on this island – there are several pretty little coastal villages.

The island is green and grand, with sheer cliff faces rising from the sea along the west coast. Covered with pines and scrub, this land plays host to lacy green and brown snakes, which move with disturbing speed, but luckily always away from noise or movement.

The lush landscape changes in the far south into a barren rocky promontory rising high over sheer white cliffs. A lighthouse now stands on the highest point called Sappho's Leap, where the poetess is said to have taken her last bow when spurned in love. It is no place for anyone who suffers from vertigo. The best beaches are the shingle bays of Agios Nikitas and Agios Ioannis in the north, and Vasiliki and Rouda in the south, or the Yiro sandspit outside Lefkas town. But this island is more notable for its scenery than its beaches.

There are regular caiques and buses to Nidri on the east coast, from where you can have a ringside view of the yachts, jetties and armed guards on Skorpios, the private island of Greek shipping tycoon Aristotle Onassis. The king is dead, but daughter Christina still makes occasional visits.

Travel

ROAD   4 buses daily from Athens Kifissou Street terminal (7 hrs).

BOAT   3 ferries a week to Ithaca and Cephalonia; also to Patras.

Cephalonia

The island of Cephalonia, or Kefallinia – there must be at least six ways of spelling it – is shaped like a jigsaw puzzle piece, which divides it into three or four regions. The abiding impression of the whole island is that it is green, mountainous and fertile. It is also well populated, with five ports and scores of neat red-roofed villages peeping through its pine, cypress and olive trees and surrounded by the most productive vineyards in the Ionian isles.

Cephalonia's blossoms and vines are reminiscent of Zakinthos; its greenness and grandeur of Corfu, which it slightly exceeds in size. But Cephalonia is not so neat as Zakinthos, nor so rich as Corfu in history, culture or beaches. The main towns are drab, but tourists are still thin on the ground in most parts of the island and there are treasures for those prepared to look for them.

The new villages and tidy rows of prefabs at the main port of Sami are the legacy of the 1953 earthquake, which hit Cephalonia harder than the other Ionians. It may also account for the dusty flat appearance of Argostoli, the capital, and its twin town of Lixourion, linked by a half hour ferry crossing across the Gulf of Argostolion.

The island's airport is served by direct flights from both Athens and London. Visitors arriving by air land seven kilometres south of Argostoli and fly in over the island's best beaches, nine or ten successive coves of brown sand at Livadi, Plati Yialos and Irina. The southern beaches are a joy to swim off and account for the three large beach hotels and half a dozen small pensions that have sprung up close to the coast road.

Argostoli is an honest, but dull, town with numerous hotels, a huge fruit market and a mole road across its own narrow gulf. It also has an improving bus service to all parts of the island from the market, and two shops with scooters for hire at around 900 drachmas a day.

The road to Poros is the best on the island. It goes past the sandy beaches of the south coast to the well preserved mediaeval castle of St George at Kastro. Then it dips towards the coast at Peratata and Karavados, where there is a left turn for the monastery of the patron saint, Gerasimos, and a right turn for the attractive little beach restaurant at Gallini. There is another good sand beach further along the coast at Lourdata.

The beach of Poros is long and shingle and the village offers some of the best eating on Cephalonia, plus scenic walks around the coast to the delightful harbours of Skala and Katelios, both with shingle beaches. There is also an easy ferry connection to Kyllini on the Peloponnese. The road from Poros to Sami is of the first class riverbed variety, though it passes through spectacular scenery lined with fruit trees, and beehives which produce the island's crop of delicious thyme-honey.

Sami has smartened up a lot in the past ten years and has almost lost its earthquake look. It has a long pebble beach and a colourful harbour with regular, though long, ferry connections to Corfu, Paxos and Patras as well as Cephalonia's northern port of Fiskardo. Also within walking distance of Sami are two of the most spectacular caves in Greece, Drogarati, bristling stalactites like teeth, and Melissani. The latter is the closest thing to the Styx and the entry to the Underworld I have ever seen. It comprises a lake in a crater part open to the sky, which throws strange lights through the water illuminating wriggling eels in shallow parts. Our boatman had a dog in the bows of his craft, which I patted and jokingly called Cerberus. At that moment he gave a long, lingering howl that echoed for a minute through the cavern. I like to think I had innocently stumbled across a descendant of the animal Odysseus encountered when he passed this way 3,000 years ago, but it is more likely that his canine vigil in the bows had been interrupted by a couple of surfacing eels.

Fiskardo, in the north-east of the island, is a classic Greek island port with an enclosed harbour ringed by colourful restaurants and cafes. It is a popular port of call for yachts from Corfu and has a number of pebble beaches nearby. The road south from the northern spur of the island to Lixourion passes Assos, a spectacular little port with a castle on its peninsular, then snakes high above two gleaming sand and pebble beaches on the Gulf of Myrtou. Both are backed by high cliffs, but accessible by stony track. The one called Myrtou is the most spectacular and remote, but the other, Agios Kyriaki, has a tiny restaurant and rooms.

Lixourion, with its ferry crossing to Argostoli, is the ugliest town on the island and short of good pensions. But, even in this region there are good things to be found. A few kilometres north at Variko lies a long, gentle brown sand beach with superb restaurant and rooms. There is another reddish beach on the south coast at Agios Georgios, near Kounapetra, a rock which is said to sway with the tide. It is also worth making the trip across the western spur, occasionally served by bus, to the monastery of Kepourio perched high on the cliffs above the sea. Its earlier population of seventy monks is reduced to only four, but they make visitors welcome.

Cephalonian restaurants rarely serve retsina. The island has so many good wines of its own, notably the flinty white Rombola, Manzavino and Calliga. All are a bit overpriced in bottles and usually local wine by the carafe is the cheapest and the best.

A less savoury feature of the island is that curse of the Ionian Isles – oil. This scars many of the white pebble beaches black with man-made tar, but fortunately it seems to be fairly rare on the prime sandy strips.

Travel

FLIGHTS	International charter flights At least 1 flight daily from Athens (45 mins).
BOAT	3 ferries daily from Patras (4 hrs); 1 daily ferry to Ithaca.
SPEEDBOAT	Daily summer speedboat service to Patras.

Ithaca

The island kingdom of Odysseus lies snug in the lee of sprawling Cephalonia. It doesn't quite fit Homer's description, though the name is enough to convey a lot of atmosphere, and it says something that the Prince and Princess of Wales chose Ithaca as their first honeymoon anchorage in Greece.

It is the steepest and rockiest of the western Ionian isles, supporting little more than olives, vines, the odd cornfield and herds of goats. But, in no way does it 'face the wide ocean' – though it might have looked that way to a traveller like Homer in 800 BC.

Ships from Corfu, Cephalonia and Patras put in at Vathi, the main port and capital. A natural horseshoe harbour surrounded by hills and olive groves, the red-roofed town fits as though tailormade for it. It is a friendly place with good cheap kebab stalls, bars and restaurants along the quayside.

Vathi is not believed to be the harbour of Odysseus, or his capital, though you can find signposts to both at Aetos and Stavros in the north of the island. A cave within walking distance of the port is designated the 'Cave of the Nymphs', where Odysseus hid his going away presents from the Phaecians, but looks no different from many other caves on or near the coast.

'Arethusa's fountain' describes a small spring in the south. This apparently threw Byron into raptures and is worth visiting on a light evening, if only for the walk.

Ithaca boasts pretty shingle beaches at Aetos and Sarakiniko across the headlands from Vathi. Also at Agios Ioannis on the coast road, and near Frikes and Kioni in the north, though the oil of passing ships scars most of these beaches. Polis has a pretty harbour with a pebble beach and sometimes doubles for 'the harbour of Odysseus'.

An occasional bus runs the length of the island, but there are bikes and mopeds for hire, and caiques run around the coast in summer. Although Ithaca is extremely close to Cephalonia, it is about an hour's journey by island steamer.

Travel

BOAT   3 ferries a week from Patras; connections with Cephalonia and Corfu.

Zakinthos

Unlike Cephalonia, Zakinthos – or Zante, its Italian name – was rebuilt in some style after the 1953 earthquake that levelled most of the town. The best of the Venetian remains seem to have been preserved.

This island has style in everything. It strikes you the moment you set eyes on the harbour and main town from the plane, or the ferry or speedboat from Kyllini or Patras. The impression sticks firm on a trip along the south and east coasts – the only ones accessible by bus and car, as the west is high and rocky. Zakinthos has beauty in its pine trees, its flowers and its sandy beaches. These beaches line the sheltered south coast and can be found intermittently on the east coast of the island at places like Alikes in the north and Tsilivi, Krioneri and Argassion nearer the town.

Laganas, beyond the airport, is the most popular beach resort on the south coast, but Porto Roma near Vasiliko is the prettiest – a curve of sand with a thatched restaurant at one end fringed with trees. There are other slightly less accessible strands in the lee of the south-east cape beyond Vasiliko and at Kalamaki, Vrontoneron and Limni. Giant tortoises live in the surrounding pine woods and they frequently risk their lives or their shells on the roads. Yet more remote beaches can be found by diverting from the Porto Roma road.

There are buses to most main points along the three main coast roads, south, east and north, and bikes and scooters can be hired in the town. The town of Zakinthos is graceful with well-ordered green squares, palm trees and pink and beige Venetian buildings along the quayside. There is also the ruins of a fort above the harbour and this garrisoned British soldiers during the Ionian mandate over a century ago.

The town boasts a dozen good restaurants on picturesque squares and terraces where strolling musicians regularly revive the Venetian occupation at its best with local cantades or folk-songs accompanied by guitar and mandolin. Try the Malias Fish Restaurant or stroll up the hill towards the fort where there are two restaurants with spectacular views or along the coast towards Akrotiri, a village where there are three thatched beach restaurants.

Zakinthos town has four grand churches, but the earthquake destroyed some of the best old buildings and as good places to view religious history are the town's two museums just off Solomos Square, which is named after the island's famous early 19th Century poet.

The wine and cologne are both worth sampling (at different times) and Zakinthos boasts an unusually high quota of cinemas – four at the last count. There are also three discotheques within easy walking distance along the coast.

Most of the popular beaches have rooms and restaurants, including Argassion, Tsilivi, Porto Roma, and Alikes. This applies to Laganas too, where the beach stretches for miles and serves as a road as well as a roasting place for sun-worshipping holidaymakers.

Beyond Laganas on the way to Keri is one of the wonders of Zakinthos, pitch springs which have been there since the time of Herodotus. Keri itself is worth a visit for it is the centre of a hunting area where rabbits and fowl abound. Although there was nowhere to stay the last time I visited the village, a simple cafe turned out the spiciest rabbit stew I have eaten anywhere.

The island is shaped like a lobster's claw and is renowned for its picturesque caves and healing sulphur springs. The most spectacular caves are the 'Blue' and 'Papa' grottoes on the coast near Cape Skinari lighthouse, around Agios Georgios; Gkremna on the west coast, and the 'Big'

('Megali') cave in the hills in the middle of the island.

Travel

FLIGHTS   International charter flights. Daily flight from Athens (30 mins).

BOAT   6 ferries daily from Kyllini (2 hrs).

SPEEDBOAT   Daily summer speedboat service to Patras.

Kythera

Always classed as the seventh Ionian isle, Kythera is out on its own to the south of the Peloponnese and Cape Maleas. It only seems to be grouped with the Western Isles because it fits no other group and has common historical links with the Venetians. Since it is brown and barren, with whitewashed houses, Kythera has as good a claim to being grouped with the Cyclades. It also has historical links with the Peloponnese, and strong more modern links with Australia, where many young men have emigrated during this century and before.

It is inadvisable to sunbathe topless on the beaches near Chora because of the ever-vigilant police who are more than willing to haul you up to the police station for hours of questioning.

The bus service is poor and Kythera lacks the hotels and rooms you would expect for an island of its size. This freedom from tourist development is surprising because Kythera is not lacking in beauty, and was, after all, the honeymoon isle of Helen of Troy. It is also accessible, thanks to a direct air link with Athens, a summer hydrofoil service and regular ships down the Peloponnese, which call at both Agia Pelagia and Kapsali after two and four hour trips from Neapolis and Gytheon respectively.

Both the main ports, on opposite sides of the island, have good sandy beaches in adjoining bays and there are several others as well – Platia Ammos in the north, Diakofti on the east coast, and a long pebble beach at Kastri in the Bay of Avlemona.

Chora, the capital, stands high above Kapsali with a lofty Venetian castle and breathtaking views of the two bays and the road snaking down to the port below. It is a tough walk uphill. An infrequent bus service connects the main island towns, the most regular run being from Agia Pelagia to the little market town of Potamos. Take this and get off at Dokana for a walk of about four kilometres to the fabulous Milopotamo cave, which boasts some of the best stalactites and stalagmites in Greece and the spectacular Nereides waterfall, which fills a small swimming pool where the old people of Kythera take medicinal baths in April.

Travel

FLIGHTS	Up to 2 flights daily from Athens (1 hr 5 mins).
BOAT	2 ferries a week from Piraeus (10 hrs); good ferry connections with south Peloponnese. 1 weekly ferry to Crete.

HYDROFOIL	5 times a week during summer months from Zea Marina (near Piraeus).

Elafonissos and Antikythera

Ships to Neapolis often call at the simple and oddly-named isle of Elafonissos. Here at the port is a passable beach, a restaurant and a friendly harbour front. There is a better beach in the next bay.

En route for Crete, there is also a weekly ship from Kythera to Antikythera, but this rocky islet, which is mainly populated by goats and has only one small bare village, hardly justifies the long journey.

Travel

BOAT	ELAFONISSOS 2 ferries a week from Piraeus; connections also with Kythera and mainland Peloponnese.
BOAT	ANTIKYTHERA Up to 2 ferries a week from Kythera en route for Crete.

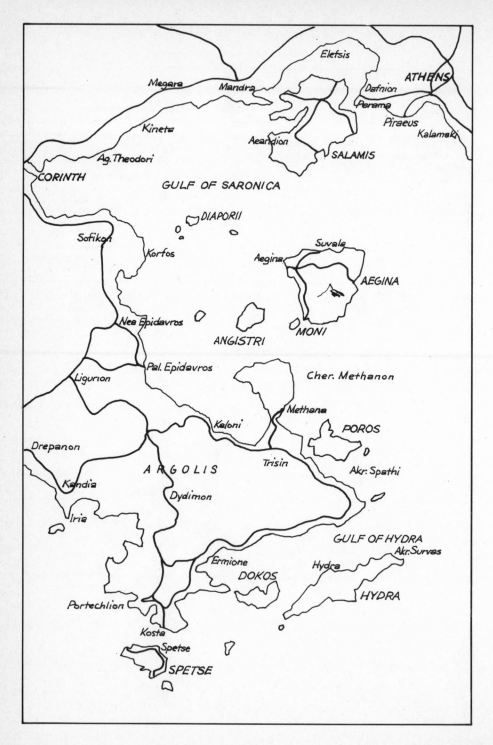

54

Saronic Islands

Around half of the ferries that plough in and out of Piraeus harbour do a quick shuttle service to the five main islands of the Saronic Gulf – Salamis, Aegina, Poros, Hydra and Spetse. All are near enough for a day trip from Athens and the boats with exuberant names like 'Portokalia Helios' (Orange Sun) and 'Saint Nectarios', have docking procedures, timetables and refreshment facilities that put the big island ships to shame. In addition to the ferries, all these islands (except Salamis) are now served by a speedy hydrofoil service from Piraeus and Zea Marina.

Salamis

Salamis, site of the famous sea battle that put an end to the second Persian invasion of Greece, and Xerxes' ambitions of avenging the defeat of Darius, is the first major island in the Saronic Gulf. It can be reached either from Piraeus or from a few kilometres along the coast at Perama, where flat-bottomed ferries run a ten minute service across a narrow strait.

Salamis is a mixture of green and brown, with dockyards running down to shallow bays. The villages are white, but not particularly pretty, while the few swimming places, which I have heard described as 'lovely sandy beaches', are poor. They are either of the pebble and stone variety or as muddy as they are sandy.

Travel

BOAT   There are up to about 70 short crossings daily from Piraeus or Perama. Perama is reached by bus from Athens (20 mins).

Aegina

There is a ship about every half an hour to Aegina, second nearest of the Saronic quintet, and the journey takes one to one-and-half hours (30 minutes by hydrofoil). This is the busiest isle in the Gulf and ships calling there seem to disgorge hundreds of people at a time on to the bustling quayside. But Aegina has a knack of absorbing them all without ever looking crowded. Island buses, bicycle hire shops and painted carriages drawn by plumed horses, vie for attention with pistachio nut sellers, restaurants and the most colourful fruit and vegetable market in Greece.

The far spur of the harbour has a little wedding cake church dedicated to the sailors. From here, too, are daily caiques to Aegina's two satellite isles of Moni and Angistri. Both islands boast shiny yellow beaches and pine woods. Moni has a camp site and Angistri has rooms and restaurants around its sandy coves.

Aegina town itself has a passable sandy beach to the left of the harbour. There is another small one at Perdika down the coast opposite Moni and a long stretch of gently sloping sand at Aegina Marina. Twenty minutes bus ride across the island, Aegina Marina rivals the main town as a holiday centre with a string of hotels and restaurants overlooking the beach. A short walk, bus or donkey ride from here lies the temple of Aphaia Athene, built on a high rock in the pine woods. It dates from the 5th Century BC and has two concentric rectangles of Doric columns.

Travel

BOAT   Service about every 30 mins from Piraeus (1 hr 30 mins).

HYDROFOIL   Daily service from Piraeus (30 mins).

Poros

Poros lies third on the Saronic route and so close to the Peloponnese coast that it sometimes seems that two ships will have difficulty passing each other in the narrow channel. It is over two hours from Piraeus by ship; less than an hour by hydrofoil.

The port of Poros rises like a pyramid of white cubes from the calm blue waters of the channel. Its quayside teems with cafes, restaurants, hotels and the Greek navy. Benzina water-taxis skip across the straits to the mainland, supplementing the regular ferry crossings and giving a Venetian flavour to the place.

If you eat on the quayside, which boasts a good variety of restaurants and tavernas, you will be entertained by regular ship arrivals and departures – the two are almost simultaneous – accompanied by bells, speakers and the whine of engines churning into reverse thrust. The bay immediately flanking the port, which is just swimmable, contains a naval school and the old battleship 'Averoff', flagship of the Greek navy until her well-earned retirement at Poros in 1945.

Perhaps Poros as an island doesn't quite live up to the initial promise of the port, but there are delights for those prepared to hunt for them, which is not hard on an island only four miles across and long at its furthest extremity. The little peninsular with the port on its tip is called Sferia. You can walk around it in an hour, taking in the beaches of Neorion, Limenaki tis Agapis ('little harbour of the lovers'), and Askeli Bay.

There are also two discotheques, a water-skiing school and windsurfing school on the peninsular.

Kalavria is green and quiet, and contains many shingle coves fringed with pine trees, as well as the monastery of Zoodochos Pigi ('spring of life') and the remains of a temple of Poseidon.

The beaches of Poros are not the stuff that dreams are made of, but the island has attracted a number of British package tour firms in recent years. This is partly explained by the lively port, an abundance of accommodation, and easy access to the Peloponnese via Galata just opposite. On the Peloponnese there are some good beaches along from Galata and, an easy bus ride away, are the port of Methana, the ampitheatre of Epidavros, ancient Troezene with its Frankish castle, Lemonodassos ('the lemon forest') and the waterfall at Devil's Gorge.

Travel

BOAT	Frequent ferry service from Piraeus (2 hr 30 mins), and from Poros harbour to Galata on Peloponnese mainland.
HYDROFOIL	Daily service from Zea Marina, near Piraeus (1 hr).

Hydra

Around three hours by ferry from Athens – but only half that by the 'Flying Dolphin' hydrofoil – lies the bare, brown island of Hydra. It, too, is not spectacular for beaches, but what the island lacks in natural appeal it has largely made up in an amazing picturesque port, colourful history and great character.

Hydra's bare cliffs end in a galaxy of colour in the port, where stately mansions rise up in browns, pinks, greens and blues topped by bright red roofs. Cannon stand at the harbour mouth, signifying the island's important seafaring past and its role in supplying ships in the Greek War of Independence in the 19th Century.

It is not surprising that artists, film directors and sun-worshippers flock to this island. Hydra has launched many fine paintings and was the setting of the fifties film 'Boy on a Dolphin'.

Hydra now has the makings of a T-shaped road to both ends of the island, which runs to two pretty monasteries, but not much else.

There are beaches ten minutes to the right and left of the town, reached by foot or boat. These are of the better pebble variety and Mandraki beach contains the island's windsurfing school. But many people take to the boats to Costa, Ermioni or Porto Heli on the Peloponnese, or settle for smooth rocks by the harbour. On these rocks, a strong odour of sun oil prevails throughout the summer, and it is not unusual to see devoted worshippers of Apollo using large sheet mirrors to maximise their tans.

Yachts flock to the harbour of Hydra and it has a cosmopolitan flavour in summer, when the waterside restaurants flaunt lobsters by the dozen, the shops are decked with expensive furs and the five discotheques stay crowded until the early hours.

Travel

BOAT   Frequent service from Piraeus (3 hrs). Also ferry connections to Ermioni on Peloponnese mainland.

HYDROFOIL   Daily service from Zea Marina, near Piraeus (1 hr 15 mins).

Spetse

More tranquil than Hydra and as different from it in appearance as Hydra is from Poros, Spetse lies around four hours by ferry, or two hours by hydrofoil, from Piraeus. It is a pine covered island, with sandy/pebble coves around every corner of the coast. The most popular are Zogeria in the north and Paraskevi and Anagyri in the west.

Spetse has a ring road of sorts, plus horse drawn carriages which clatter along its narrow concrete streets with a haunting rhythm. There are bikes and mopeds for hire, but the island is small enough to be walked around and across, through fresh smelling pine woods where tortoises roam. East of the town and south of the island you can see the private islet of Spetsapoula,

owned by the Niarchos shipping family. To the west lies a school and pine coast that inspired John Fowles to write 'The Magus'. His island of Phraxos was based on Spetse when it was in no way the tourist isle it is today.

Spetse is mainly white in the traditional style of green islands and it has a tiny enclosed harbour crammed with fishing smacks and some first class restaurants. It is busy and popular with British package tours.

The main port around the Dappia, is a maze of restaurants and bars and also contains three discotheques and two cinemas, giving Spetse far more night life than is found on most Greek islands. This area also contains mounted cannons, a little museum and a bust of Bouboulina, a fierce Amazon of a woman who stirred the locals to start the Greek War of Independence by sailing their fleet against the Turks in 1821. The port is busy and noisy by night. It rocks until early in the morning and sleeps late. But there are quiet spots to stay around the town and a few rooms in the north of the island at Vrello and Agios Georgios.

There are no cars on the island, but there are occasional buses and the horse-drawn carriages will transport you along the ring road.

Anyone not happy with the beaches of Spetse can find two long smooth sandy stretches half an hour away on the Peloponnese at Costa and Porto Heli. Caiques make regular crossings as well as sailing round to the island beaches.

Travel

BOAT   Frequent service from Piraeus (4 hr 30 mins). Also caique service to Costa and Porto Heli on Peloponnese mainland.

HYDROFOIL   Daily service from Zea Marina, near Piraeus (2 hrs).

The Sporades

North of Evia and east of Volos and Pelion are a group of four green islands. These share pine-clad slopes, red-roofed white houses and a steamer service from Kimi on Evia in the south and from Agios Constantinos and Volos in the north. In turn both mainland ports are served by buses from the Liossion bus station in Athens. Skiathos also has an air link with the capital for those who don't want to spend a day on buses and ships, plus some direct flights from Britain.

Skiathos

The air links with Britain and Athens symbolise Skiathos' place as the number one tourist isle in the Sporades. It has grown into that role gradually over the past twenty years, thanks to a pretty port on a pine-covered peninsular and an endless series of sandy beaches in 57 varieties, which stretch all the way along the south coast to the well-publicised Koukounaries. Unfortunately there is only one town on Skiathos and this is geting a bit too developed for comfort. There is also but one main road, so you need to walk to lose the crowds.

A mile of fine sand with pine trees and a lake behind, Koukounaries is as pretty and comfortable as it ever was, but let no-one think this is a place to get away from it all. There is a Xenia hotel at one end of the beach, two or three restaurants charging fairly fancy prices in the middle, and a landing stage served by regular boats from Skiathos port nine kilometres away along the coast.

Boats go daily around the island to another of Greece's best-known beaches – Lalaria cove, blessed by nature with dazzling white pebbles and an open archway in a rocky promontory that juts out into the sea like a prehistoric monster. The same boats often call at Kastro, which as well as a lovely beach, offers a spectacular climb up a cliff to a Byzantine monastery, a frescoed church and the remains of a castle.

The harbour of Skiathos town is crowded and cosmopolitan with good restaurants, nightlife and buses to the nearby beaches.

It also has bicycles for hire. Not far down the coast is a villa development and water-ski school. The peninsular jutting out from the harbour boasts cannon and a concrete area which sometimes transforms into a dance floor in summer. When it is not working, there are three discotheques in the town, which makes Skiathos a lively place in mid-summer; visitors seeking quiet and cheaper prices should stay on the edge of town or a short way outside towards Megali Ammos or Achladias, the nearest beach resorts on either side, both of which also have good restaurants.

Other beaches worth visiting are Platanias, Vromolimno and Troulos off the road towards the crowded Koukounaries. Then there's the curve of Krassa bay, which serves as Skiathos' main nudist beach, and is but a short walk across the headland from the Koukounaries bus stop. Also try Mandraki and Aesilinos, both more deserted and call for a caique or a stiff walk across to the north-west coast of the island. On the north-east coast the best strands are at Megali Ammos and Megali Yialos.

Skiathos is the most easily reached of the Sporades via a three-hour boat journey from Agios Konstantinos or Volos. It is a little more than an hour from Loutraki on Skopelos, and two hours from Skopelos port.

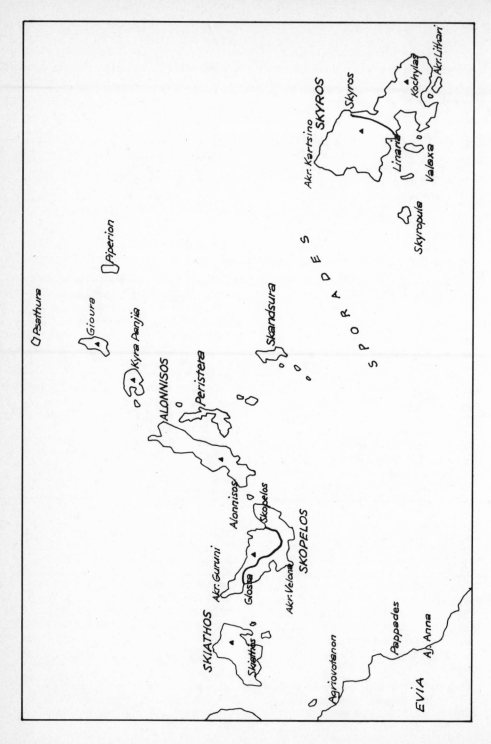

International charter flights. 3 flights daily from Athens (50 mins).

BOAT Regular daily crossings from Volos or Agios Konstantinos. Buses from Athens, Liossion bus terminal, to Volos (5 hrs 15 mins), Agios Konstantinos (2 hrs 30 mins). Skiathos also has ferry connections with other Sporades islands and Thessalonika.

Skopelos

The next port of call for the Sporades steamers en route from Skiathos is the less developed island of Skopelos. It means 'the reef' in Greek and Skopelos is certainly less sandy than its northern neighbour, but it is equally pine-coated and somehow more solid than Skiathos.

The port is a delight. It glistens white, rises high and is crammed full of churches. Not to mention tavernas, where raki and tsipoura are strong favourites and local retsina pours thick like glue from a barrel. The port has no nightlife other than its restaurants along and off the quayside, but there are pretty daytime walks to the Venetian castle above the town. Nearby Ambeliki has the ruins of an asklepion, or hospital, by the seaside, and Agios Konstantinos, has a shingle beach and ancient watchtower.

You can swim from a shingle beach near the harbour, walk across the island to beaches at Agnontas and Staphylos, where small restaurants nestle into the pines and beneath the cliffs, or take a bus along the coast to the twin ports of Loutraki and Klima at the far tip of the island.

Walkable from the bus, which plies the island's only real road, are some moderately good pebble beaches at Panormos Milia, Elios and Klima, all with restaurants. Glossa is the main village on the northern spur of Skopelos, and a beautiful one built in the woods high above the coast. But a better place to stay is its

port of Loutraki, an honest little fishing harbour with pebble beach. From here ships run a shorter route to Skiathos.

Travel

BOAT Twice-daily ferries from Volos (4 hrs 30 mins) via Skiathos. Ferries 3 times a week from Kimi on Evia (3 hrs 30 mins).

Alonnisos

Third of the Sporades Islands and only half an hour's journey around two capes from Skopelos, is Alonnisos. Almost undeveloped in the sixties, with a pretty square port at Patiri and a main town that suffered bad earthquake damage in 1965, Alonnisos has blossomed with tourists in recent years due to the siting of beach hotels along its shores.

It is a healthy half hour walk from the port to the main town and to a series of cove beaches which tend to be pebble, like the long curve of the romantically-titled Chryssi Milia – or 'golden apple' bay, the Marpounta holiday village and Steni Valla. The only other way of getting around is by boat, the quickest and best way by far.

The island swept on to the tourist track in the early 1970's when a French architect built the Club Marpounta. With accommodation for 200 people, tennis court and dance floor, the Club straggles up a pine-clad hillside on a peninsular between two bays. These bays provide reasonable swimming, one from pebbles and the other from tons of fine yellow sand which were imported to give Alonnisos its first proper sand beach.

Ships from Skopelos bound for Skyros pass close by Marpounta on their way into Patiri, giving passengers a grandstand view of the holiday village and the clients a daily glimpse of the world beyond the pines and the green-grey bulk of Skopelos across the straits.

For the best swimming you have to take a caique from the harbour or from Club Marpounta to the nearby islet of Peristera

which has more exotic beaches than
Alonnisos.

Travel

BOAT   Daily ferries from Volos (5 hrs),
3 times a week from Kimi on
Evia (3 hrs); daily to Skiathos
(3 hrs) and 3 times a week from
Agios Constantino's (5 hrs).

Skyros

Four hours south of Alonnisos, but little
more than two hours from Kimi on the east
coast of Evia, Skyros is where Rupert
Brooke chose to be buried and where the
film 'Cry in the Wind' was filmed.

Skyros is bursting with character. It is
famed for tiny ponies, miniature furniture
and for local peasant dress – the old men
wear baggy black pants and sandals and
the women black dresses, embroidered
blouses and patterned scarves.

The main village is sprinkled like salt down
a steep hillside high above the coast.
Originally to protect it from pirates, the
style of housing is peculiar to Skyros, with
white cubes topped by flat gravel roofs.
Strangely, a similar type can be seen in
parts of the Moorish coast of Spain, around
Almeria province, making you wonder
about the daring and skilful seamanship of
the early Greeks.

The village is surmounted by a castle and
the paths up there and from the coast to the
village are nearly all terraced steps on
which donkeys make better progress than
people. At night many villages open the
doors of their houses to let passers-by
admire gleaming rows of copper pans and
galleried beds.

Like Alonnisos, Skyros has made rapid
progress in the past decade. Thanks to its
closeness to the mainland and its unique
character, the island is now invaded by
crowds of tourists in the summer, including
many Greeks from Athens. The main
village has straggled right down and
around the sandy beaches that run around
the coast at that point, fewer villagers wear
traditional dress and the main street which
used to be close to deserted noon and
night, now throbs with movement and
carousing round the clock.

It can be too much, but there is a saving
grace. The port of Linaria, opposite Evia, is
not so pretty, but is less developed. It is a
good place to stay with the view to
exploring the west coast of the island and is
close to some equally good sandy beaches.

A final note – Skyros is a drinker's island. It
seems to consume half the retsina and beer
production of all Greece every evening.

Travel

BOAT   Daily service from Kimi on Evia
(2 hrs), and 3 times weekly from
Volos (12 hrs) via other
Sporades islands.

North-East Aegean Islands

Twelve islands that strangely lack a group name or clear identity curl around the north and east Aegean, hugging first the coast of northern Greece and then the Turkish mainland. They are usually called simply the north-eastern Aegean isles, but could in modern times easily acquire the unwanted title of 'The Disputed Isles'.

This is the area where Turkey and Greece disagree over subsea and continental shelf oil rights, and the five isles nearest to Turkey have all had stronger links in the past with that country than most other islands of Greece.

All these north-east islands are more fertile than the central Aegean isles and most are bigger. They are no less easy to reach than the Cyclades thanks to a string of airports on the big four – Lemnos, Lesbos, Chios and Samos. Thassos, which is much closer to Greece than to Turkey, has good ferry links with the northern coast at nearby Kavala, a town with a direct air link to Athens.

Thassos

Surrounded by sandy beaches, covered with pine trees and green vegetation, and only a bit over an hour's journey by regular flat-bottomed ferry from Kavala, Thassos is the most northerly Greek isle of all. It is a natural magnet for campers and motorists from northern Greece, and from western Europe, who enter Greece via Yugoslavia and Thessalonika.

Fortunately, the island has a ring road with regular bus services and ample accommodation for both casual visitors and long-stay campers in the neighbourhood of Thassos port in the north, Limenaria in the south and the second port of Prinos. Thassos port has cars and bicycles for hire

and a number of disco bars that rock the waterfront on summer evenings.

The whole island is welcoming and easily accessible, but Limenaria, the farthest place from the ferries and Thassos port, is a particular delight. The port has great character and within half an hour's walking distance are a number of appealing beaches in sandy coves.

On the east coast there is a long sand strand at Makriammos, which usually attracts favourable comments, and there are others at Aliki, Kinira and near Potamia. But, Thassos is an island where you are never far from a good beach.

Travel

BOAT   Up to 11 ferries daily from Kavala (1 hr) and 10 crossings daily from Keramoti (45 mins).

Amouliani

Only 15 minutes journey by boat from Ouranoupolis, or by regular ferry from Tripite on the main Thessalonika-Ouranoupolis road, Amouliani is visited by few foreign tourists. But, it is a little gem of an island, with superb beaches all round its shores, and so close to the mainland that the journey can hold no horrors for nervous seafarers. The views of the Halkidiki mainland are beautiful, with the craggy contours of Mount Athos dominating the eastern skyline on a clear day.

The main port is in traditional white house and red-roofed Halkidiki style, spoilt just a little by the modern building of bigger concrete summer houses. There are good rooms to rent and three or four restaurants. There are also two discos, but they seem rarely in use.

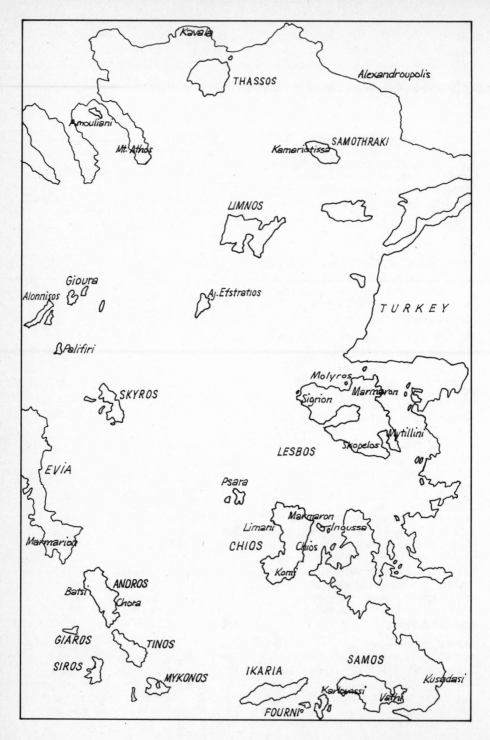

POROS

The Monastery of Zoodochos
Pigi (Spring of Life), Poros.

SPETSAI

Spetsai's harbour, crammed
with fishing smacks and
colourful restaurants.

SKIATHOS

Skiathos' coastline is surrounded by splended sandy beaches.

SKOPELOS

Skopelos, where the port is
full of churches.

Comprising mainly of undulating hills covered with olive trees, figs and vines, and with none of its sandy coves more than an hour away from the port, the island is ideal for walking. But, for those who don't want to walk even that far, take the local taxi, which in Amouliani comes as a wooden cart pulled by a frisky grey horse.

For the best beaches, walk beyond Limani to Agios Georgios, Megali Ammos or Aliki, the last lying across the headland and having a campsite and beach restaurant. There are other good beaches along the south coast at Galapigada and Garagatsi, and on the short west coast at Phalca and Trutovoul.

Travel

BOAT   Daily ferry services from Tripite and Ouranoupolis.

Samothraki

Tucked away in the far north-east corner of the Aegean, and very close to the Turkish isle of Imbros, Samothraki seems to be coveted more by the Turks than the tourists. All due to a hint of oil around the nearby sea boundary between the two countries. As a result, there is a garrison of Greek infantry stationed in the castle capital of Chora, a few kilometres uphill from the pretty port of Kamariotissa.

There is no good reason, other than perhaps the military presence, why Samothraki should have been so neglected compared with its bigger neighbour, Thassos. It has a fair range of beaches, with some sand along the coast from Kamariotissa, and the scenery is green and lush, reaching up 5,500 feet to Mount Fengari, the highest point in the Aegean.

Paleopolis, further along the coast with regular bus connections, is the site of the Great Sanctuary, and Therma has a spring and curative baths in a wooded setting. It, too, has a pretty, though pebble beach. Walk in the opposite direction along the coast towards Lakkoma and you will find some pretty and abandoned swimmable coves.

The famous statue of the Winged Victory, now in the Louvre, was found in Samothraki by French archaeologists and the site is still a beautiful sanctuary with Ionic columns proudly standing in a majestic green setting.

Samothraki is reached by ferry from Alexandroupolis in about two hours, or from the nearby isles of Thassos and Lemnos. The island connection is preferable because it avoids a long journey along the coast, and Alexandroupolis, which is a seedy border town teeming with troops and overpriced hotels.

Travel

BOAT   Daily service from Alexandroupolis (2 hrs 30 mins). Ferry connections with other north-east Aegean islands.

Lemnos

With an airport and one of the prettiest ports in Greece at Myrina, at first sight Lemnos looks like a gem among Greek islands. Unfortunately, the rest of the island is peculiarly lacking in character.

Myrina boasts a fortress on a high promontory and sandy bays on both sides. It also has a good road to Moudros, the main town on the south side of the island.

Moudros stands on a huge enclosed bay, so protected that the sea appears to be a land-locked lagoon. It was here that the British fleet found a secure anchorage in World War One before the ill-starred landing on the Dardanelles. But the coast is muddy and the town is amazingly dull.

Lemnos has good sea connections from the mainland via Evia and Skyros, and from Kavala and Samothraki in the north and Lesbos to the south. The best beaches away from Myrina are along the coast near Thanos in the south-west of the island.

Myrina has three first-class restaurants along the harbour and an equally good shopping centre for fruit, yoghurt and pastries, making it a good place to stay. There is a beach hotel around the northern bay curving out from the town, but there are two cheaper places along the waterfront of the port and another along the southern beach.

Travel

FLIGHTS   Up to 2 daily flights from Athens (45 mins). Daily flight from Thessalonika (40 mins).

BOAT   Lemnos has good ferry connections with Alexandroupolis via Samothraki; Kavala; Thessalonika; Kimi via Syros; and Lesbos.

Agios Efstratios

Unsung by the poets and so far ignored by the march of tourism, Agios Efstratios is a short stop for ships linking Evia and Lemnos. Disembarkation is by small boat.

The main village is not the pretty wedding cake style found on many Aegean isles. The neat rows of single-storey bungalows are characteristic of a Greek island that has suffered earthquake damage. There are no roads across the island, and places to stay are hard to find, though there are a couple of rooms in the village hostel and the islanders sometimes rent their houses. All this helps to explain why Agios Efstratios has been used to exile political offenders far away from the mainstream of Greek life during periods of dictatorship.

Yet the island has a quiet charm and great friendliness when you get to know it. It also boasts some of the best sandy beaches in the Aegean, reached by walking between half an hour and two hours over hills and headlands.

There are no restaurants on the distant beaches, though the one along the beach by the village does a surprisingly good line in roast meat and is far more imaginative than the old-fashioned bar/cafe on the harbourside.

A promontory above the village supports one of the most fascinating graveyards I have seen in Greece, where it is possible to trace the unusual and slightly grisly burial customs of the Orthodox Church, open coffins and all.

Travel

BOAT   Ferries from Kimi on Evia and Kavala, via Lemnos.

Lesbos

Sappho's isle of Lesbos, (Lesvos or Mytileni), is the third largest in the Aegean. Resembling a piece of a jigsaw puzzle, with two huge sandy bays cutting deep into its underbelly, it is served by regular ships from Piraeus, Chios and Lemnos, as well as having a direct air link with Athens and some international charter flights.

It is a grand, high-reaching, fertile island. Herds of horses, donkeys, pigs and goats graze on flat meadows around the twin gulfs on Yera and Kalloni, olive trees abound, and the hills around the 3,000 foot bald peak of Mount Olympos are covered with pine forests, wild flowers and scented herbs. There are also good beaches for those prepared to travel.

Lesbos supports large populations in its main towns of Mytileni and Mithimna (or Molyvos) – both called after the daughters of the mythical first settler, Macar – while Plomari, Kalloni, Agiassos, Moria, Adissa and Polihnitos are all bustling villages. They have red roofs, multi-coloured houses and light industry, and all consume an unusually large amount of local ouzo, which the islanders claim is the best in Greece.

Mytileni, the main port which forms a horseshoe around a big natural harbour, is not an appealing town, though it has a reasonable brown sand beach and its castle is spectacular. The beach is below the castle east of the port. On the way you pass the Lesbos Statue of Liberty, a miniature of that in New York, and also a statue of Sappho, the world's first poetess, who gave the word 'lesbian' to the world by penning love odes to her female students. Away from Mytileni, Lesdos has some grand bays surrounded by green woods and olive groves. It also boasts one of the prettiest villages in Greece – Molyvos. This lies beneath a high mediaeval castle, and stately houses of many colours spill down a hillside until Molyvos ends in a pretty miniature port. It is reminiscent of Lindos on Rhodes and the harbourside by the 'Sea Horse' inn has featured on the sleeves of many records of popular Greek music. Molyvos is also a favourite spot for painters.

Molyvos is a good eating scene and there are amazing views from the walls of its Frankish castle, but it lacks a good beach and is overflowing with tourists in summer. With your own transport, it is better to stay at Petra 5 kilometres down the coast, which has a long brown sand beach. A spectacular church perched on a high rock gives the village its name and lends a lot of character.

Those who want somewhere quieter than Molyvos should hire a scooter in Mytileni and explore the beaches of Neapolis and Kalimari near the town, or the southern peninsular around Kratigos and Agios Ermogenis, both have reasonable coves. The coast road north of Mytileni makes an easy scenic run as far as Mandamos and has a smattering of swimmable beaches beyond the warm spring resort of Thermi, but all are stoney. The most spectacular sandy coves are found in the south and west of the island.

The south is lush and forested. It boasts a good sandy beach at Aghios Isidoros close to Plomari, which is the ouzo capital of the island and has a lively night-time scene at restaurants and cafes along its cobbled lanes beside one of the island's many rivers. But the most appealing beach in the south is the long, pine-fringed sand stretch at Vatera, south of Polihnitos, where there are rooms and restaurants. The bus, unfortunately, only goes as far as Vrisa, 4 kilometres away. There are other sandy beaches on the Gulf of Yera south

of Skala Polihnitos, at Skala Kalloni, and north of Achladeri.

Skala Eressos in the west has a long sandy beach with windsurfing and a lively tourist scene, but the best beaches in this area are a series of silver sand coves around Sigri, which also has a well-preserved little castle and the remnants of fossilised trees – often grandly described as a "petrified forest" in a cluster in the village square, in a **rocky cove on the far side of Megalonisi** island which straddles the bay, and in the hills below Ipsilou Monastery, another religious place perched on a high rock.

A pleasant two-hour trip to Megalonisi costs around 250 drachmas a head from Sigri harbour.

There are two other picturesque monasteries on the west road to Sigri and Eressos, that of Limonas beyond Kalloni and Pytharion close to Erressos, while Skala Sikaminias in the north has a pretty chapel on a rock in the sea.

There are buses from Mytilent to all the resorts.

Travel

FLIGHTS	International charter flights. Up to 4 flights daily from Athens (45 mins); 5 weekly flights from Thessalonika (1 hr 40 mins).
BOAT	Ferries 4 times a week from Piraeus (14 hrs); other ferry connections with Lemnos and Chios. Ferries to Ayvalik on Turkey.

Chios
Curl-shaped Chios looks as though it has just drifted away from the Turkish mainland. The distance between the two is only a few miles and the main town of the island shows, in its architecture and sweet shops, signs of centuries of Turkish occupation. Chios has a big, bustling port set on a curving bay and bursting with oriental pastries, Turkish delight,

preserved fruits, ouzo and those mastic products which are deemed a speciality in this part of Greece. The buildings stand tall with red roofs facing the Turkish coast across the narrow straits.

Like Lesbos, Chios has an airport, daily ships from Piraeus and sea links with the other east Aegean isles. But, like its northern neighbours, it is disappointing for its size, though it does have some spectacular countryside with high hills standing back from the coast and fertile plains fronting the sea. Again, like some other islands, the military are much in evidence on the coast facing Turkey, despite an intermittent daily boat service from Chios to Chesme.

South of the town are the famous mastic plantations. These produce a dull-tasting grey gum which, when combined with sugar and flavouring, makes chewing gum and some of the local liquors. Legend says that this part of Chios is the only place in Greece where mastic will grow, and even attempts to grow it in the north of Chios have failed.

There is a long sand beach at Karfas just south of the town, but after that you have to travel some way for good beaches. There is a pebble beach at Kakaraktis and shingle at Komi and Emborion in the far south. North of Chios town the pretty harbour of Langhada has another stretch of shingle, but perhaps the best beaches are at Lithion, Nagos and Skala Volissos on the west coast.

Chios has a proud past and it is worth visiting the 11th Century monastery. Called Nea Moni, it is set in wild rugged hills eight kilometres west of the town and is maintained by only a tiny portion of its original complement of monks. The monastery of Agios Minas near Pirgi is of much later date, but is revered as the site of a horrible massacre in the early days of the War of Independence.

Kato Pana on the south coast has the remains of a temple of Apollo and Emborion has an ancient acropolis above the beach. Regular boats go from Chios town to the pretty satellite isle of Inoussa

and from there and Limnia to the other nearby isle of Psara.

Travel

FLIGHTS   2 flights daily from Athens (40 mins).

BOAT   Ferries 5 times a week from Piraeus (10 hrs); weekly ferry from Rafina and Thessalonika; also ferry connections with Lesbos, Samos and Syros. Intermittent ferry connection with Chesme (Turkey).

Inoussa and Psara

You can take a short boat trip from Chios harbour to the peaceful little island of Inoussa. Here, lying between Chios and Turkey, you can find freedom from noise and the military. All with the added bonus of good sandy beaches around every corner of the coast. Inoussa has two small pensions and is a lovely place to stay a few days.

There are also excursions from Chios to the quiet isle of Psara. This, too, has a sprinkling of good beaches and a pretty little harbour. Plus a strong line in festivities, notably commemorating Greek independence as a result of some sea action fought off the island in 1824.

Ikaria

Ships bound for Samos from Piraeus, or sometimes on the Rhodes to Samos route in summer, stop at Ikaria, a rocky island which supports large flocks of goats and a lively trade in their hides.

Men on Ikaria often carry knapsacks on their backs made up from whole goatskins with the legs acting as straps and the tails hanging down behind.

From autumn through winter the strong winds blow and Ikaria is not so well served by sea. Also, unlike its big neighbours, the island has no airport, even though it is called after Icarus, the first flier according to legend, whose wax wings melted in the warm sunshine above the island.

The capital, Agios Kirikos, is a grand port backed by high hills. It has a number of small hotels and swimming is from rough pebbles and stones. Better is Therma, a pretty spa resort along the coast, a short boat or bus ride away, which boasts five warm mineral springs, more hotels, a sheltered pebble beach and, reputedly, the most radioactive springs in Europe.

The best places for a long stay on Ikaria are the pine-fringed bays at Armenistis and Yialisea on the northern coast, reached by bus and/or taxi via Evdelos. There you can find tavernas and rooms and miles of deserted sandy coves for swimming in.

Nas, 3 kilometres west of Armenistis, has a pretty pebble beach, campsite, restaurant and the remains of an ancient harbour.

The interior has an air of peace and grandeur. Those longing for a sandy beach within easy access of Agios Kirikos can find regular boats in summer going across to the nearby Fourni isles. Boats also run along the coast from Agios Kirikos to Pharos and Keramos, tiny villages which offer better swimming than the port. For land transport, there is an infrequent bus service across the island from the square in Agios Kirikos.

Travel

BOAT Ferries 4 times a week from Piraeus (10 hrs); other ferry connections with Samos, Lemnos and Lesbos; also to Patmos and other Dodecannese islands.

Fourni

Two islands with one name more often visited by yachtsmen than island-hopping tourists, Fourni deserves to be better-known. The main island is shaped like a question mark and has two small villages, Fourni and Chrysomilia, at opposite ends of a long curving bay that describes the loop. The port of Fourni has an unusual tree-lined main street which is traffic-free.

A daily small boat from Agios Kirikos makes the tree-lined harbour in one-and-half hours. There are both pebble and sand beaches across the headlands on both sides of the harbour.

The best beach near the port is Kaba, reached over the headland to the east via the windmills. It is sandy and boasts a small taverna with good home cooking.

Samos

It was once called 'the Isle of the Blessed' and there's no doubt that Samos does enjoy a rich blend of good things. It is prettier than its three big neighbours – Lesbos, Chios and Ikaria, easier to explore, thanks to a good ring road around the island, and more accessible.

In common with the other big eastern Aegean islands, Samos has an airport on a flat coastal strip near Pythagorion, and now has direct flights from Britain. It has ships from Piraeus, and acts as a sea junction between the Dodecannese and the north-east Aegean islands with a summer hydrofoil link to Patmos. Finally, it has the only consistent daily island links to Turkey. Before the invasion of Cyprus, it was easy to travel to the Turkish mainland from Lesbos, Chios, Kos, Samos and Rhodes. Not so nowadays, which makes the daily short crossing from Samos port to Kushadasi all the more valuable, even though it now costs nearly 1,500 drachmas one way.

Samos is rich in architecture, agriculture, history and beaches. Its only limitation is the frequency of buses, which is not brilliant. However, it has become possible in the past few years to rent motor-bikes, and these open up the island at whim for around 900 drachmas a day.

The two main steamer ports are Samos and Karlovassi, both in the north, but occasional boats go from the prettier port of Pythagorion on the south side of the island to Kushadasi, and the tiny islets of Agathonissi and Arki.

Samos port, merging into Vathy higher up the hill, is the biggest town with white houses and bright red roofs typical of the island. Karlovassi sprawls and lacks character. Pythagorion and Kokaria are prettier places to stay, though the former is notably more expensive than anywhere else on the island.

Hora, once the Turkish capital, is a good place to stay for those who find Pythagorion too busy or expensive. Ircon is another and has a reasonable beach. Between Pythagorion and Samos are the two limpid bays of Possidonion and Psili Ammos, easily reached from Samos and offering close views of the Turkish mainland only a kilometre or two away. They both have first-class beaches, which can be reached by a stiff walk from Samos port.

The road along the north coast winds through pinewoods with a long series of swimmable pebble and sand coves below, but it is at the western end of the island that the best beaches are to be found. There is a superb crescent of golden sand at Iamatike Pige, a few kilometres beyond Karlovassi and another in the south beyond Marathokambos called Votsalakia. These are two of the best beaches in Greece and are now linked by a meandering coast road around the western tip of the island.

Pythagorion has the history. It is called after the great mathematician, who was born there. Nearby you can see the remnants of the huge Heraion temple of the goddess Hera, regarded as one of the wonders of the Ancient World, as well as the Efpalinion underground aquaduct that ran for 1,000 metres through the hills. The single standing column of the Heraion and the open jaws of the Efpalinion speak volumes for the 6th Century BC dictatorship that built both. Pythagorion and Samos have archaeological museums containing statues, reliefs and vases from the golden age of Samos and also from nearby Asia. Samos also boasts a Byzantine museum, attesting to its glories in that period. It is complemented by many grand monasteries around the island. The two oldest are the Annunciation, built on lofty Mount Kerkis, and Our Lady of the River, near Karlovassi. Both date from the 10th Century.

All around the island are areas where pinewoods give way to terraces of vines and Samos wines are superb, resinated or plain, sweet or dry. The sweet wines are invariably a rich brown colour and the dry usually lighter yellow, though a few reds are also produced. There is a pretty little tale that the god Bacchus taught the Samians to make wine in return for their help getting rid of the Amazons, who had been rude to him.

Travel

FLIGHTS	International charter flights. 2 flights daily from Athens (45 mins).
BOAT	Daily ferries from Piraeus (12 hrs); good connections with other north-east Aegean islands as well as the Dodecannese. Daily summer ferry to Kushadasi in Turkey.
HYDROFOIL	Summer service to Patmos and Kos.

The Dodecanese

A highly evocative word that simply means 'twelve islands', the Dodecanese are the glittering group that occupy the south-east corner of the Aegean, bounded by Turkey in the east, Crete in the south, the Cyclades in the west and Samos in the north.

To make it all confusing, there are fourteen major inhabited islands in the group and the biggest, Rhodes and Kos, were not original members. The Dodecanese are mainly greener and more fertile than the Cyclades. They are bound together by a common history, which is closely linked with the Crusades and an Italian occupation up to the 1940's. Today most still have mediaeval castles rising above their ports, plus low rates of Taxes. Karpathos and Kassos seem the odd two out, both more closely linked to Cretan culture.

Patmos

The first port of call in the Dodecanese coming from Samos or Mykonos, Patmos seems a link with the Cyclades rather than the closer eastern Aegean isles. It is small and brown, with neat white houses and enclosed little sand spit bays.

It does, though, have the typical trademarks of the Dodecanese – an arched Italianate harbour authority building on the quayside and a castle overshadowing the main town on the hill behind the port. In the case of Patmos however, the castle is unique. It is, in fact, the monastery of St John the Divine, built to the memory of St John and his two year exile on the island in which he received and wrote the Revelations, the last and most lyrical book of the Bible.

The monastery was built by a lone monk called Christodoulos. He settled on the island in 1088 when it was uninhabited, and shortly afterwards had the whole of Patmos gifted to him by an edict of the Byzantine emperor. That edict hangs proudly in the monastery along with one of the richest collections of treasures to be seen in Greece. The monastery itself is a fascinating little village of winding streets, stairways and chapels with fine frescoes depicting John's sufferings at the hands of the Romans.

It stands above what must be one of the most precious and authentic shrines of Christianity – the cave where St John received the revelations through three cracks in the ceiling, and dictated them to his pupil Prohoros. Now, surrounded by a religious school, the cave is on the left side of the road that leads up two kilometres from the port to Hora and the monastery. Strangely, it is not well advertised and you could easily miss it in a hurry. I had to disturb a monk at his classes to persuade him to unlock the door of the chapel that is now built onto the cave, and I am sure that many coach loads of cruise ship passengers visiting the monastery never see it at all, although it is depicted on many postcards. A sad thought is that this, one of the true shrines of religion, is being neglected at the expense of the more worldly buildings and relics that celebrate it.

But Patmos is much more than a memory to St John. The village of Hora surrounding the monastery is one of the oldest in the Aegean, with pretty winding streets and little squares. The main square has two above-average restaurants.

The island is shaped like a compressed octopus. As a result, most parts are within walking or biking distance and there are stone and sand beaches between almost all the tentacles.

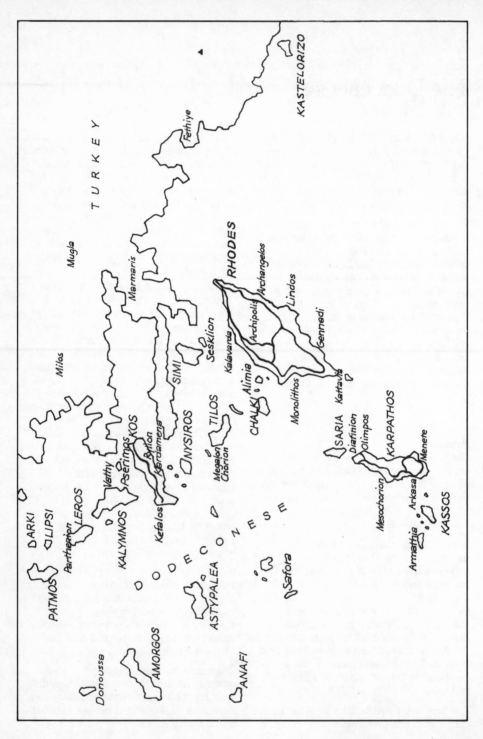

Skala, the port, has several beaches (two stony), but there are better ones within an hour's walk, or ten minute bus ride, at Grikou and Agriolivado. Grikou is a lovely little village with two hotels, two good restaurants and five beaches to choose from. The bus to the north comes down from Hora through Skala to Kambos, which is also a pretty little village, but with a stony beach. The best beach on the island is Psili Ammos, a smooth sand stretch in a deep bay to the south, reached either by boat from the port or a spectacular walk south from Hora or Grikou. Others worth swimming are Meli, Netia, Livadi, Stavrou and Lambi.

Everywhere you walk on Patmos you see churches and monasteries, and they lend to the quiet of the place. It is tranquil all the time, even surprisingly when the cruise ships arrive at Skala for a few hours almost every day and the gift shops along the quay suddenly burst into life.

Like most of the Dodecanese, Patmos is also a cheap island, and there is a shop in Skala renting bicycles and motor bikes for considerably less than you would find elsewhere in Greece. In the summer, boats ply from the port to the little isles of Fourni and Lipsi. Lipsi makes a relaxing day out for swimming and lunch.

Travel

BOAT   5 ferries a week from Piraeus (8 hrs); daily ferry to Samos; ferry connections with Leros, Kalymnos, Kos and Rhodes. Also with Naxos and other Cyclades islands as well as Kavala and Thessalonika.

HYDROFOIL Summer service to Kos and Rhodes.

Lipsi
At first sight, you would think that Lipsi had more blue-domed churches than houses, but this rocky little isle, one hour from Patmos and the same from Leros, has a thriving little town with two pensions.

The island has no roads and is blissfully quiet. There are three sandy strips of beach around the curving bay that contains the harbour and others can be found by walking along the southern headland. Lipsi is served once a week by the Dodecanese steamers and makes a good day trip from Patmos and Leros by caique.

Travel

BOAT   Twice-weekly ferry connections in summer with Patmos, Leros and other Dodecanese islands. Caiques to and from Patmos and Leros.

Leros
Leros sprang to fame as the main prison camp isle for political offenders during the military dictatorship of the colonels (1967-1973). But, that was a second coming, for there was fierce fighting on Leros in the middle years of the Second World War. Thanks to its sheltered bays and harbours – some say the best in the Aegean – it became a naval base for the Italians during the war and the inhabitants still talk of a brief period of British occupation.

Two huge guns here inspired Alastair Maclean to write 'The Guns of Navarone', though the high cliffs of Lindos and hundreds of willing donkey men resulted in the island of Rhodes being the actual setting for the film. The steep mountains and Castle of the Knights at Platani help the imagination to work on such events, but mountains give way to fertile green oases near the coast and the houses of Platani, the capital, and Lakki, its coastal rival, are the white cubes seen on all nearby Aegean isles.

Lakki has Italian architecture, but does not unfortunately match the wonders of Rhodes and Kos. Its harbour is the busiest on Leros and stands at the fulcrum of a huge bay with palm trees along the quayside. From there to Platani or Agia Marina, is only three kilometres, but is a trip that often has to be made on foot or by taxi. There is an occasional bus which runs the length of the island, and bikes can be hired.

The best beaches are near Partheni at Agia Marina and Pantele, at Gourna, and on the far southern shore of the island, though all are shingle and do not compare with those of most neighbouring islands.

Leros shares with its bigger neighbour, Kalymnos, the practice of sending ships annually to North Africa on sponge fishing expeditions, and their divers to an early grave.

Travel

BOAT   4 ferries a week from Piraeus (10 hrs); ferry connections with Kalmynos, Kos, Rhodes, Patmos and Samos.

Kalymnos

Best known as the home of the Greek sponge fishing fleet, Kalymnos is a busy island. The big square port of Pothia bustles with noise 18-20 hours a day and is flecked with the blues and greens that colour many big harbours in the eastern Aegean. The town climbs upwards amphitheatre-style from a deep bay, and its architecture portrays the start of red roofs in the Dodecanese chain.

Like Leros, the public transport system leaves a lot to be desired, but Kalymnos has a marvellous solution; a well developed public taxi system, which is common in Turkey and the Middle East, but sadly rare on Greek islands. You can go along any main road quickly and cheaply with a black granny on your lap and a slight whine from the back axle.

The east coast of the island north of Vathy is mountainous and inaccessible, though Vathy itself is worth a visit, being a pretty white fishing harbour set at the apex of a fertile valley surrounded by barren brown rocks. A good road runs along the west coast to the resorts of Kantouni, with its shingle beach; Myrties, the prettiest village on the island, ablaze with cubist houses, green shrubs and flowers; Massouri, with a gentle sand beach; and Arginonta and Emborio further north.

Only two-and-a-half kilometres from Pothia, near Horio, is an old walled city called Kastro which contains the remains of nine churches. Two other trips worth making for sun and sea are to the tiny beach resorts of Vlichadia and, by boat from Myrties or Massouri, across to Telendos island. A healthy walk from Kalymnos is to the cave of the seven virgins, also called the grotto of the nymphs, where the luckless seven fled to escape pirates and lost themselves in its deep passageways. Zeus also has a pretty grotto dedicated to him up in the mountains near Agia Ekaterini.

There are few traces of the sponge fishermen in summer, as they are away working the coasts of North Africa. Their womenfolk wait anxiously, as well they might. The diving equipment used has a First World War look about it and few divers live past their forties. If they do, they age prematurely. Sad, but true.

Travel

BOAT   Up to 8 ferries a week from Piraeus (14 hrs); Good ferry connections with Rhodes, Kos and Leros. Weekly connections with other Dodecanese and Cyclades islands.
Caiques can be hired for the short crossing between Kalymnos and Kos.

Telendos

Telendos has good sandy beaches and this statuesque little islet can be reached in 15 minutes by small boat from Myrties or Massouri on Kalymnos. It has a small fishing village and some delightful isolated coves.

In the straits off Telenda village an ancient town lies buried under the sea. You can see the outline of walls and houses from the surface on a calm day, but locals say it has never been explored. The theory is that Kalymnos and Telendos were once joined together, but were separated by an earthquake in 535 AD, which launched the town into the sea.

Travel

BOAT About 15 minutes by small boat from Kalymnos (Myrties or Massouri).

Kos

Kos is a mini-Rhodes. It has the same Italian-style waterfront and Castle of the Knights, an airport with direct international flights, a verdant interior and some good sandy beaches around its shores. There is also a sprinkling of interesting archaeology, with the famous Asclepion, 2 kilometres south of the town, where the Hippocratic oath was first taken in the 5th Century BC.

It is more doubtful that Hippocrates taught medicine beneath the spreading plane tree in the town, but the way it fills a little square with its 12 metre girth lends some credulity to the story. It is hard to believe, too, that the long leaved lettuces of the same name originated here, though Kos is greener than many of the Greek islands.

Kos town is neat, clean and cheap – a legacy of the Italians and the special customs status granted to most of the Dodecanese isles. Nowhere can you find bottled spirits (usually in litres) and wines at cheaper prices than Kos. It gives the Vinko label added appeal, especially as most of the measures are big ones too. Can that be why the town has such a frenetic atmosphere at night?

Kos town is prettily laid out with cool gardens and cafes stretching along the promenade and harbour. It has shady trees, a healthy string of good restaurants in and around the main square fronting the harbour and competitive hotels. Kos town contains the remains of a market place, baths, villa and temple of mixed Greek and Roman parentage on an open green area that is more of a public park than strict archaeological site.

Bicycles and scooters can easily be rented in the town and the island has good roads; many places are within a day's cycle ride and more than a few within an hour's pedalling distance. One of the latter group is the Asclepion, which is a remarkably well preserved terraced building at the end of an avenue of cypress trees. It has baths and temples, plus a good view of the Turkish mainland, rising only a few kilometres from the eyes of this fish shaped island.

Also close is the bay of Agias Fokas, one of the best sand beaches near the town, with the health resort of Thermes a few kilometres further along the coast. As well as a warm beach for bathing, Thermes used to have a friendly pet goat called Marilena, who, in answer to her name, would scuttle over the rocks and try to eat everything in sight. Sadly there was no sign of her on a recent visit.

There are other sandy beaches close to the town on the north coast at Marmarion, Lambi and Tigaki. On the same coast, but a healthy cycle ride away, is the good beach and attractive fishing village of Mastihari. But, like so many of the larger Greek islands, Kos has a rough and a smooth side. Here it's the northern coast that tends to have the rougher beaches and seas.

On the south coast and only six kilometres from the airport, Kardamena is the fastest developing tourist resort around, with hotels, tavernas and a long, long stretch of sand, where you can nearly always walk far enough to get away from the crowd. The village, swelling yearly with the advent of British package tours, has scooters and bikes for hire, regular caiques crossing to the nearby island of Nissiros and a wide range of restaurants. Two places serving particularly delicious food are the Tavernaki at one end of the village and the Laikon, on a terrace above the beach, at the other.

The best beach on Kos is at Kamares (also called Agios Stefanos after an ancient church on the seashore) east of Kefalos. Here there are dunes, soft sand, pine trees, a fishing port and a choice of places to stay. Six kilometres from Kefalos, and a little further from Kamares, is the pretty monastery of Agios Ioannis.

As well as having good air connections, Kos is better served by sea than any other Dodecanese island, other than Rhodes. Rhodes and Patmos are both only four hours sailing time away (1 hr 30 mins by the summer hydrofoil service). Also, since 1980 there have been regular excursions across the narrow straits to Bodrum on the Turkish mainland, but they are expensive.

Travel

FLIGHTS   International charter flights. Up to 3 flights a day from Athens (50 mins). Daily flight from Rhodes (45 mins).

BOAT   Daily ferry to Rhodes. Good ferry connections with Patmos, Leros, Kalymnos, Nissiros, Samos and Mykonos. There are also up to 8 ferries a week from Piraeus (14 hrs). Occasional excursions to Bodrum on Turkish mainland.

HYDROFOIL   Summer service to Rhodes, Patmos and Samos.

Pserimos

Kos is a good base from which to visit other Dodecanese islands like Nissiros, Tilos, Kalymnos, Leros, Patmos and Rhodes. One tiny rocky island even nearer that makes a delightful day trip is Pserimos, only an hour's sailing from Kos harbour. Pserimos has a tiny village on a sheltered creek containing one of the best sandy beaches in the Dodecanese. The village boasts two cafe/restaurants and a small pension. The island also offers some superb quiet walks, so it makes a good retreat for two or three days away from bustling Kos or Kalymnos. It is about the same sailing distance from both.

Travel

BOAT   Daily caiques (summer) from Kos. Caiques also go from Kalymnos.

Nissiros

Tiny Nissiros is another haven of peace and quiet. The volcano that towers over it has long been extinct, but it has given the island a fertility it might not otherwise enjoy. The land around the crater is emerald green and there are hot sulphur springs bubbling away.

The capital and harbour of Mandraki, which sees regular caiques from Kardamena on the Kos coast opposite, as well as twice weekly ships from Kos town, is a pretty fishing village with winding streets and byways. There's a bus service from Mandraki to the volcano. It's a trip that should not be missed. The sights are spectacular, especially when walking around the large crater.

The beaches of Nissiros are apt to be rocky, but there is a stretch of sand to the right of Mandraki and some spectacular pebble beaches around the headland behind the monastery and Castle of the Knights which lie above and beyond the harbour. There is also a sandy beach at Pali, to which an occasional bus runs. Further up the coast is a crumbling old spa complex, complete with hot baths, cafe, and hens and goats feeding beneath spreading trees.

Taxis, some of them Land Rovers, do a lively business up to the hill villages of Emborio and Nikia and to the volcano. And, in summer, occasional boats go to the tiny nearby islet of Yiali opposite Mandraki, where there is a good sand beach.

Travel

BOAT   1 ferry a week from Piraeus (over 20 hrs). 2 ferry connections a week with Kos town, Tilos, Symi and Rhodes. Regular caique service to Kardamena (Kos).

Astipalea

Astipalea stands out from the other Dodecanese islands like a bridge between them and the Cyclades. Craggy hills and a landscape burnt brown by the mid-Aegean sun and winds, are the main island features, but Astipalea also has green fertile strips which produce the local wine, fruit and vegetable harvest.

The island is shaped like a balloon that has been squeezed hard in the middle to make two separate halves, joined by a narrow strip halfway. At that point Astipalea is less than 100 yards wide.

A well-preserved Castle of the Knights towers over the port and the Hora and this, together with a row of six windmills, give the twin villages great style. The castle also gives its name to local Kastellani wines, spirits and soft drinks. The port has half a dozen hotels and restaurants, plus a small strip of sandy beach. But, the best bet for those staying in this part of the island is the village of Livadi, reached by a stiff, but spectacular, uphill walk to the Hora and then down to the bay beyond.

There are no buses on Astipalea, but it is worth taking a taxi 12 kilometres along the coast to Analipsi or Maltezana, a remote oasis of fertility which has rooms, two small restaurants and a peaceful sandy bay. From there it is easy to explore the northern end of the island on foot, though a boat (if you can find one) is probably the best way of getting to the village of Vathi.

Because it is quite hard to get to, the whole of Astipalea is peaceful, quiet and uncrowded; an important bonus in a world of mass tourism.

Travel

BOAT   Up to 3 ferries a week from Piraeus via Amorgos (over 20 hrs).
2 ferries a week to Kos, Kalymnos and Rhodes.

Tilos
Less than an hour and a half's sailing south of Nissiros, Tilos is almost as unlike its nearest neighbour as it could be. It has hills, but no dominating volcano, a large natural port at Livadia and good beaches.

Tilos is three to five sailing hours from

Rhodes, depending on the route taken. It is a good get-away-from-it-all island, but not strong on the trappings of modern civilisation. There are only two simple cafe/restaurants in the main port of Livadia, one beach taverna at Agios Antonios and, up to last year, no buses or even regular taxis plying the 15 kilometres between Livadia and Agios Antonios. It is possible to hire three wheeler trucks or small boats to make the trip, but don't plan to tarry in Mikro Horio or Megalo Horio. Both have the air of deserted villages. Mikro Horio makes a good evening walk across the hills from Livadia to look at a modern Greek 'ghost village'.

Livadia itself has a pebble beach, but the best sand can be found at Agios Antonios near Megalo Horio, and reached by walking over rough tracks or small boat around the coast. Much of the coastline resembles that of Patmos, although the local castle does not match the monastery of St John.

Tilos is also one of the Dodecanese islands where women are apt to don pretty needleworked dresses for feast days, weddings and homecoming parties.

Travel

BOAT   1 ferry a week from Piraeus; 3 main ferry connections a week with Rhodes, Symi, Nissiros and Kos.

Simi
One of the most stunning sights in the Aegean is the harbour of Simi. The tall thin buildings of the port rise several storeys up to red roofs, blending with each other and a host of churches, as though they had been planned and built simultaneously for a film set.

Simi is separated by narrow brooding straits from the Turkish mainland opposite. It is mostly rocky and its main businesses are fishing, boat building and sponge diving. All the more surprising that the port should be so colourful and well designed, but it obviously reflects past glories when

Simi was the home of sea captains and had a thriving sponge fishing industry.

Egiali has most of the action on the island and is the centre for most British package tours, which have done a lot to open up the island to the outside world. A discotheque plays nightly during high summer across the bay at Nos beach. Back in the port there are lively restaurants and bars and a rough road connection to Horio, the real capital of the island.

With old houses on winding streets and pebble mosaics of ships and mermaids, Horio lies about 15 minutes walk from the harbour. There's now a road across the spiney backbone of the island to the monastery of Panormitis, or you can approach it from the coast by boat. But, it is worth visiting just to see the carved wooden altar screen and a silver and gold icon. Ten years ago the only food available there were sea eggs, but time has brought some rewards.

Alas, both the beach there and at Egiali are stony and weedy, though the water is usually clear. But there are beautiful walks around the coast – to pretty remote beaches. Pebble gives way to smooth shingle at Pethy and Nos, half an hour away around the headland on foot or by boat from Egiali harbour. There is another shingle beach at Manzouri, about the same distance from Panormitis.

Simi is served once a week by the regular Dodecanese ferries and there are day trips from Rhodes in summer.

Travel

BOAT   2 ferries a week from Piraeus; daily summer service with Rhodes; weekly ferries to other Dodecanese islands.

Halki

Halki is one of nine islets clustered round the west coast of Rhodes. Though nearby Alimia has a better harbour beach, Halki stands out from them all because it is the biggest island of the group and has a daily ferry from Kamiros Skala on Rhodes (two

on Sundays and Thursdays). The journey takes just over an hour.

Halki is a haven of peace and, because of its size, readily walkable. Just as well, because there are no buses. But, what Halki lacks in transport, it makes up for in a grand port dominated by two high bell towers, multi-storey houses and an Italianate harbour police and post office, all built in the same style as the island of Simi.

Halki, too, once spawned a fleet of sponge-fishing vessels, and their wealth built the single island road – a thin concrete structure which streaks up to the Castle of the Knights and then ends in mid-hill on the way to the Monastery of Stavros and the best sandy beach on the island.

Beaches appear to be few on Halki, yet are there if you look hard enough. The most popular one near the port is a tiny silver sand strip by the road to the castle. This boasts a restaurant and rooms, but gets crowded in no time. There is a lonely pebble beach, with sand in the water, less than an hour's walk to the north across the first bay beyond the port, and another similar one barely ten minutes along the coast to the south. But, the best beaches are under the Castle cliff and beyond it. These call for a boat ride, costing an exorbitant fee of around 1500 drachmas a trip, no matter how many passengers there are.

Halki is short on accommodation, with only three or four small pensions, but it is well served by restaurants. There are four in the main port and, to my mind, the one immediately opposite the ferry mooring serves the best spaghetti bolognaise in Greece. Fish is cheap on the island, despite unusually fierce competition from a flock of brown cormorants who nest along the shores, and can stay under water longer than any spear fisherman.

When walking, look out for the occasional snake. They tend to flee at the first sign of human life, but it is worth taking a little care to avoid the fate of a Greek woman tourist I met who suffered a painful, though hardly fatal, bite on the ankle. When she sought medical help, she was told with typical

Hellenic fatalism 'It's not a snake-bite. There are no snakes on this island'.

Travel

BOAT   Daily ferries from Kamiros Skala on Rhodes. Up to 2 ferries a week from Piraeus and onward connections with Rhodes. Reverse connections with Karpathos, Kassos and Crete.

Kastelorizo

How tiny Kastelorizo, lying snug in the lee of the Turkish coast and nearly fifty miles east of Rhodes, has stayed an undisputed enclave of Greek territory is a minor mystery of modern Greece. However, its very remoteness attracts many foreign holidaymakers, who make the long twice-weekly crossings from Rhodes.

There is a slight air of tragedy about Kastelorizo. A legacy of its turbulent history, with invasions and incursions by marauders of every age ending with the Italians during the Second World War, when the island was depopulated by evacuation. Geography also plays a part since the island is only a mile from the Turkish coast, yet never makes contact with it. There are only a little over 200 islanders left and they are subsidised by the Greek government or are emigres retired from the USA or Australia. The port is full of ruined houses, testifying to a grander past.

Kastelorizo, or Megisti as it is also called, has only one real village. This is the extraordinarily pretty port of white red-roofed houses with Italianate archways, lying at the end of a narrow rocky bay.

Its history has given it a magnificent castle above the harbour, which gave the island the name Kastelorizo ('red castle'). There is also another more ancient castle called Palaiocastro, dating from the Dorians above that. This is reached by a stairway via four pretty white churches, and a fascinating little museum.

The island is not strong on beaches, but there is a stretch of sand at Agios Stefanos.

The nearby islet of Agios Georgios has a good beach and boats ply the 20 minute journey from the harbour during the summer months. They also make a half-hour trip from the harbour around the coast to the blue grotto, which is one of the most spectacular of its kind in Greece.

Travel

BOAT   1 ferry a week from Piraeus, via Rhodes (over 24 hrs).
Up to 2 other ferries a week during summer from Rhodes.

Karpathos

A long, narrow island about the same size as Kos, Karpathos is both mountainous and fertile. It is also now easily accessible, thanks to regular ships between Crete and Rhodes, and a sandy air strip. The latter is served from Rhodes by a daily Skyvan plane which looks a bit like a prewar bus with wings, but makes an admirably smooth landing even in high winds.

The southern part of Karpathos is accessible by bus or scooter, which can be rented in the port of Pigadia, a colourful little harbour village with ample hotels and restaurants. From there you can take a good road south as far as the airport, passing a number of good beaches on the way, notably Ammopi, a beautiful spot where three sandy coves lie side by side with rooms and restaurants on the middle beach. Ammopi is becoming a sophisticated little resort in its way and there is a choice of both accommodation and bathing.

There is another more remote beach at Makri Yialos near the airstrip. The road around the south coast then becomes a pebble track and winds around to Arkassa, a pretty village on the west coast which has a good surfing beach nearby. Go north via Piles and there is another sandy stretch near the tiny village of Lefkos, but be warned that these are roads for the adventurous.

An easier tarmac route goes north of Pigadia, around its long curving beach, then turns inland and uphill to the beautiful village of Aperion. Up here are three other villages strung in a row across the backbone of the island – Volada, Othos and Piles. This is a road full of surprises. Aperion clings to the side of a gorge where green trees add to the exotic nature of the tall buildings. Two tiny cafes have outdoor tables in a distinctly Alpine setting.

You can take a poor coastal track north from Aperion as far as Spoa, where the villagers rarely seem to see foreigners or buses. Then descend a winding track to a charming little seaside spot called Agios Nikolaos, which can offer simple food and lodging. On the way are two good swimming places, Abata and Kyra Panagia. What you could not do until recently is to go north to Diafani by road. Even now the extension which has been in the building stages for several years remains a tricky journey with plenty of heavy lorries and grit piles in evidence. Fortunately, there is an easy alternative – a ship along the coast. Although the beach at Diafani is pebble, the trip is worth taking, for it is a charming slightly unwordly place surrounded by fertile valleys and brooding hillsides. From Diafani there is an easy two hour walk to Olympos, a majestic village set high above the sea on one side and high above a valley on the other. A less strenuous way up is by car or taxi.

Stay in this region for a while and you will be unlucky not to see a wedding or festival in local costume. The men wear dark suits and flowers, and the bride and her attendants are decked out in black skirts and pink embroidered blouses and headscarves to match. The wedding procession and party is kept going by a handful of local musicians playing local bagpipes (called tsabouna), lyra and guitar. Let no-one think these celebrations are put on for tourists or are taken lightly. A ceremony that started when I was last in Diafani went on for three days and nights, with regular processions along the beach, hour upon hour of feasting and persistent music right under the bedroom window. There was no sign that the participants ever slept – the festivities were going as strong at breakfast time as late at night. What a way to start married life.

Travel

FLIGHTS 2 daily flights from Rhodes (55 mins).

BOAT 3 ferries a week from Piraeus (23 hrs); 2 ferry connections a week with Halki, Rhodes, Kassos and Crete.

Kassos

Kassos is a tiny island whose shores are of volcanic rock, suggesting it was borne of an earthquake long ago. It is linked by ship to Karpathos, only three miles away at the nearest point, and to Crete. Kassos is another island that uses any excuse for feasting and ceremony, and every saint's day or family event calls for a party, usually in the churchyard at Fri, the main village. Then everyone on the island, including tourists, seem to be invited to dance under a sailcloth awning. Beware however, male tourists may have to pay a forfeit by dancing with the men of the village if they survive the endless round of metzes and glasses of retsina.

Kassos does not have an obviously beautiful port, though the old fishing harbour around the headland from where the big ships dock is a picture postcard scene. Nor does Kassos have distinguished beaches, though you can swim off sand in the main harbour of Agia Marina or off rocks along towards the fishing harbour. The best beach – a long stretch of yellow sand – is reached by small boat on the nearby islet of Armathia.

What the island lacks in sand, it makes up in other ways. Kassos is a great place to walk and is one of the friendliest islands in the Aegean. Cooking is also of high standard at the few restaurants around the harbour.

Travel

FLIGHTS Daily flight from Athens via Rhodes and Karpathos.

BOAT 4 ferries a week from Piraeus (over 20 hrs); 2 ferry connections a week with Karpathos, Rhodes and Crete.

The Cyclades

These are the brown isles of Greece. Scorched by the hot sun and the meltemmi wind and unprotected by any mainland nearby, they are strung across the central Aegean like a string of pearls.

They have a common ancient civilisation and common architecture in their white cubist houses and churches. There are forty islands in this group, but only twenty-four are inhabited. Four of them have airports, but the most usual means of access is by ferry from Piraeus or from Rafina and Lavrion on the east coast of Attica. The ferries run in three main directions – down the western side of the group; across the northern fringe; or across the middle with two splinter routes, one to Mykonos in the east and the other to Paros-Naxos-Ios-Santorini in the south.

Kea

Even though they are the nearest to the mainland, the islands known as the Western Cyclades seem to be off the main tourist route which runs across the central Aegean. So, Kea, though easily accessible – two hours by ship from Rafina or Lavrion on the east coast of Attica – is still never overcrowded.

The ferries put in at Korissia, a bustling little port approached between two headlands and facing the sombre remains of an old coal mine. There's another coal mine, too, on Makronissi, a long thin island circumnavigated on the way out. Despite the remains of industry, Korissia has a sizeable hotel and two good restaurants, and is a pretty place to stay. It is within easy walking distance of Vourkari, an attractive little yacht harbour.

Further away, but still within walking distance for the energetic, is the main

village of Hora (or Kea or Ioulis), linked to the port by a tarmac road with occasional buses. It has cobbled streets, a square and shops selling local wine and honey. A rough road leads down from there to beach hotels at the southern end of the island.

Most of the coastline of Kea comprises rocky coves, but there is a sandy beach between Korissia and Vourkari and another a short bus ride or half an hour's walk beyond Vourkari near Otzias. A third stretch runs below the Kea Beach Hotel in the south, divided into four coves by thin outcrops of rock and surrounded on the hillsides by white villas.

Kea is fast developing as a tourist island and both the main Korissia hotel and the Kea Beach hotel mount discotheques in mid-summer. A short walk north of Koundoros, where the Beach Hotel is situated, is the ancient city of Poiessa, with the remains of its walls and a large tower dating back to the 5th Century BC.

Ships sometimes go on from Kea to Kithnos, from where a regular line runs down the length of the Western Cyclades.

Travel

BOAT   Daily ferries from Lavrion; also from Rafina. Onward ferry connections with Kithnos, Serifos, Sifnos and Milos.

Kithnos

Served by frequent ships from Piraeus and occasional ones from Kea, Kithnos is a charming little island, with brown sandy beaches fringed with pine trees. Fertile valleys surround the two main roads, along which buses run to Loutra and Driopi on the coast, and Kithnos, the simple, whitewashed capital in the hills.

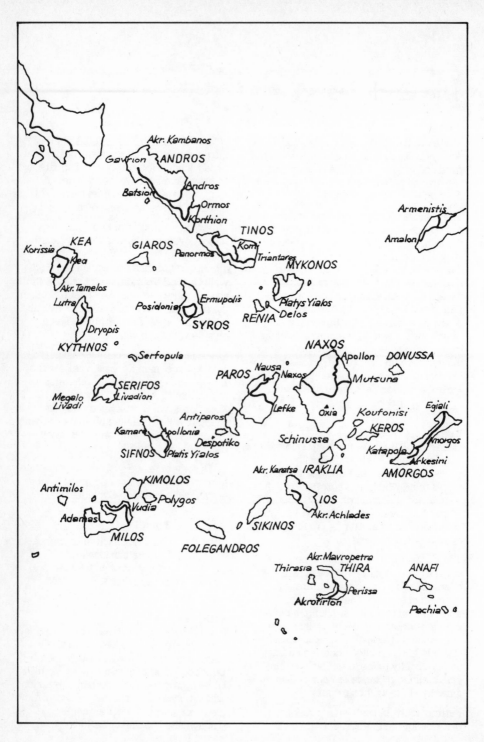

Akr. Kambanos

Gavrion ANDROS

Andros

Batsion

Ormos

Korthion

TINOS

KEA

Korissia

Kea

GIAROS

Komi

Panormos

Triantaros

MYKONOS

Armenistis

Amalon

Akr. Tamelos

Lutra

Posidonia

Ermupolis

Platys Yialos

Delos

Dryopis

SYROS

RENIA

KYTHNOS

Serfopula

NAXOS

Apollon

DONUSSA

PAROS

Nausa

Naxos

Mutsuna

SERIFOS

Livadion

Megalo
Livadi

Antiparos

Lefke

Oxia

Koufonisi

Egiali

Kamares

Apollonia

KEROS

Amorgos

Despotiko

Schinussa

Katapola

SIFNOS

Platis Yialos

Akr. Karatsa

IRAKLIA

Arkesini

AMORGOS

Antimilos

KIMOLOS

Polygos

IOS

Vudia

Akr. Achlades

Adamas

SIKINOS

MILOS

FOLEGANDROS

Akr. Mavropetra

Thirasia

THIRA

ANAFI

Perissa

Akrotirion

Pachia

82

Loutra is a spa village with thermal baths and a sheltered sandy beach, while Driopi is built out on a headland with a sandy stretch of beach beside it. But, the best beaches are a series of sandy coves within easy walking distance of the main port, Merichas, where ships call from Piraeus en route for Serifos or vice versa. Merichas has no real hotels, but plenty of rooms along the beach, plus two simple, but above-average restaurants fronting the harbour.

Look out for the surprising sweet brown wine, which is something special to a few Cyclades islands. Good, but best drunk chilled.

Travel

BOAT   6 ferries a week from Piraeus (4 hrs); 4 ferries a week from Lavrion; onward connections to Serifos, Sifnos and Milos.

Serifos
Serifos means barren rock in Greek and is always described that way. But it is a description that belies the beauty of the island, which has a warm and welcoming appearance when approaching on the ferry.

The harbour of Livadi lies at one end of a long sandy horseshoe beach fringed with pine trees and white houses. It can be a lively place with two or three good restaurants, small hotels and an intermittent music/disco scene. Perched on a rocky hill high above the harbour is the main village of Hora linked by a road that is served by an occasional bus, but can be walked in under an hour. Hora is a spectacular village with the remains of an ancient castle, old houses and a grandstand view of the bay far below.

There are a series of good sandy coves within walking distance of Livadi – Psili Ammos, Ambeli, Livasaki and Karari across the headland. There are more at Megalo Livadi and Sikamia port, linked by roads across the island, but not, alas, by bus.

Serifos is a pleasant quiet interlude between Piraeus and the more developed Sifnos, one hour to the south.

Travel

BOAT   Daily ferry from Piraeus (5 hrs); also daily ferry connections with Kithnos, Sifnos and Milos.

Sifnos
The most developed island in the Western Cyclades, Sifnos is, five or six hours sailing time from Piraeus, depending on the number of ports of call on the way. It has a startling brown landscape which contrasts vividly with the chalk-white villages and the 300-odd domed churches.

A big attraction are the island's two long sandy beaches at Plati Yialos and Vathy across the island from the main port of Kamares and reached by island buses or boat – a caique which does a circular tour via the church of Chrysopigi. Another attraction of Sifnos is the variety of the villages, which are all dramatic in appearance.

The port of Kamares stands on one side of a narrow gulf and cannot be seen from the sea until the ship has reached the entrance. It has a passable sandy beach, small hotels and restaurants along the quayside, and a fairly friendly atmosphere.

From Kamares the road climbs steeply to Apollonia, the main village of the island, and to Artemon, close by. A picturesque walk across a scorched valley brings you to the crumbling old capital, Kastro, with its Venetian castle and spotless white houses perched high on the cliffs overlooking the sea. There is a small beach below for those who can face the climb down the cliffs. Another longer walk or bus ride from Apollonia takes you to the wide sand and surf beach of Plati Yialos.

Sifnos was wealthy in ancient times, thanks ·to gold mines. The riches didn't last long, however, for the island fell foul of the Delphic oracle who demanded a golden egg as annual tribute, but was once unwisely sent a gilded rock instead. The sea flooded the mines and the islanders considered it a sign of the displeasure of the gods, but all may not have been lost. The beaches of Sifnos still have a touch of gold about them to this day.

Ferries from Sifnos run on southwards to Milos and Kimolos and in high summer caiques sometimes run east to Paros on a route that ought to be linked by a regular island service.

Travel

BOAT   Daily ferry from Piraeus (5 hr 30 mins); daily connections with Serifos and Milos. Summer caique service to Paros.

Milos

Best known for its quarries and the Venus de Milo, now in the Louvre, Milos deserves a better reputation as a holiday isle. It has an air link with Athens, some superb sandy beaches and is not lacking in charm.

The island is relatively untouched by tourism, compared with the more popular Aegean isles. Its remoteness by sea – around eight hours from Piraeus – may explain a lot; so may the stone quarries that scar many hillsides. But, as a result it offers a good refuge for anyone seeking peace and solitude with reasonable access to civilisation, a variety of places to stay and visit and good swimming almost everywhere.

Milos is shaped like a horseshoe around a big bay, which makes a wonderful natural harbour for the main port of Adamas, and also contains a wealth of calm sandy bays. It is easy to imagine that there has been a volcanic eruption similar to that on Santorini in ancient times and the sea has flooded the crater. There are certainly volcanic rocks around the shore, plus outcrops of sulphur, gypsum and obsidian, a glassy stone, from which the ancients fashioned arrow heads.

Adamas is a pretty little port with a variety of hotels and restaurants on the quayside and sandy beaches on both sides running under the shade of tamarisk trees. There

are six good sandy stretches across the bay at Emborion, a village boasting first-class home cooking and three rooms to stay in, and reached by small boat from the harbour. There is another superb deserted beach, half an hour's walk around the bay at Hivadolimni, backed by a small inland lake.

The capital, Plaka, is a picturesque village five kilometres uphill from Adamas, and connected by a regular bus service. It has a Venetian castle, folk and archaeological museums and superb views from its two dominating churches. Two other white villages share the hillside position – Tripiti and Triovossalos. The road back to Adamas makes an easy walk and there are others from Plaka to beaches at Platiena, Fyropotamos and a pebble stretch at the tiny harbour of Klima. Another walk leads to the old city where the Venus statue was found, to the catacombs of Tripiti and to a beautiful little ancient theatre overlooking the bay. The catacombs lit by candle bulbs are the most spectacular in Greece. Unfortunately, they have been shut to the public in recent years. The other main road out of Adamas goes to Apollonia, a fishing village on a big sandy bay fringed with pine trees which has two daily caiques to Kimolos.

Unfortunately, there is no bus to Agathis on the western spur of Milos, nor to Agios Ioannis on the west coast, but there are a few to the lovely sandy beach of Paliachori. Paliachori has two simple restaurants with four rooms and a hot spring a short walk to the south around a second brown sand strand, surrounded by purple and yellow stones.

There are other fine isolated beaches around the island and Milos is served regularly by ships en route for Sifnos, Kimolos or Ios. Boats go around the island in summer to the tiny Glaronissa, or gull islands, three small outcrops of land with unusual layers of spiky rock crystal. They also go to Arkoudes, Kleftiko, Triades and the cave of Sykia.

Other parts of the island accessible by road, can be reached more easily now there is a shop in the port hiring bicycles and scooters.

Travel

FLIGHTS   Up to 2 flights daily from Athens (55 mins).

BOAT   Daily ferries from Piraeus (8 hrs). Good ferry connections with Sifnos, Santorini and Ios. Also daily caique service to Kimolos.

Kimolos

There are more isolated sandy beaches on Kimolos, which is the only one of three satellite islands of Milos that is inhabited.

The caique from Apollonia passes a succession of six appealing sandy coves on Kimolos. Unfortunately, the only way to reach them is by boat or a stiff walk from Kimolos village, which is itself twenty minutes walk up the hill from the harbour. There are no rooms in the port, but the restaurant on Aliki beach has some, and there are others in the village up the hill.

The good news is that it is a pretty village with winding streets and two moderately priced tavernas. And there is good swimming both from the harbour and from smooth rocks that run north of there along two sheltered bays. The bad news is that it is not the cleanest of island capitals and a combination of donkeys and flies despoil the winding streets up through the village.

The island's best beach is a sandy strand a good hour's walk south of the port and Kimolos village. It must be half a mile long, is almost always deserted and lays good claim to being the best beach in the south Aegean.

Antimilos and Poliegos

Of Milos' other two satellite islands, Antimilos is remote and rocky and host to a rare species of chamois. But, Poliegos can be reached by boat in only fifteen minutes from Kimolos harbour for a day trip and has good swimming from three or four sandy coves facing Kimolos and the eastern shore of Milos.

Travel

BOAT   2 ferries a week from Piraeus (7 hrs) via Serifos and Milos. Twice-daily caique from Milos.

Ios

Ios is a pretty brown island mid-way between Naxos and Santorini. With windmills and tiers of white cubist houses rising up a hill over the port of Ormos, Ios has rocketed onto the tourist track over the past ten years like no other Greek island. It has three good sandy beaches, one next to the harbour at Ormos, one a healthy walk away at Mylopotamos and the other a boat ride away at Manganari in the south of the island. But, these are not enough as Ios now suffers an over-supply of young tourists swarming all over the beaches and hillsides. A new road and bus service around part of the island – from the port to the Hora and down to Mylopotamos – has helped to spread the crowds a bit, but all the beaches near the town teem with people in summer when long-term vacationing students descend on Ios to camp for a month or two, and the island fills up to the point where there seem to be ten times more visitors than the 2,000 locals. A dozen discotheques boom deep into the night transforming a peaceful Greek island scene into a frenetic Mediterranean holiday camp. Every other house seems to be a bar or club with names like 'The Foxy Fox' and 'Spiro's Bar' and not one islander seems to be employed in anything else but the tourist trade.

Ormos is a well-sheltered harbour with two headlands running from it out to sea. From there you can take a day trip to Santorini or to the much quieter little islands of Sikinos and Folegandros. Boats also run around the island in summer to Manganari beach and other coarse sand coves on the east coast like Pounda and Psathy.

Travel

BOAT   Daily ferries from Piraeus in summer (11 hrs). Also frequent ferry connections with

Santorini, Paros and Naxos. Ferry and caique service to nearby Sikinos and Folegandros.

Sikinos

One way to escape the crowds on Ios is to take a ship to nearby Sikinos and Folegandros, two little islands west of Ios which tend to be grouped together as twins, although their appearance does not justify it.

Sikinos is the nearer and more fertile. There are vineyards in the north, a thin cement road uphill across the island to Hora, the main village, and sandy beaches on both sides of the island, though the one in the east is not easily accessible by land. The island produces one of the best wines in the Cyclades, a lightly resinated white which is rarely seen away from Sikinos.

The sandy beach at Skala, the port, suggests it as the best place to stay and it is hardly overcrowded. In mid-June last year there were only a few foreigners in residence and the discotheque and hotel/restaurant just a short walk uphill from Skala had not yet bothered to open.

But Sikinos suffers in comparison with its neighbour, Folegandros. Neither the port nor the Hora is so pretty, the one accessible beach is restrictive and there is no bus service to Hora, a painful hour's walk away on a hot day.

Travel

BOAT   3 ferries a week from Piraeus (10 hrs); ferry and caique connections with Folegandros and Ios.

Folegandros

It is strange that Folegandros offers such a contrast to Sikinos, when they are so often classed together in tourist pamphlets. All that they have in common is proximity and a main hilltop village or Hora reached by a simple cement road.

Folegandros – whose name is said to mean 'rocky and arid' – is rocky and barren along much of its high shoreline which rises grandly and mysteriously 1,000 feet away from the sea in places. But, the island is also warm and friendly, with a welcoming white harbour and beach at Karavostassis and a series of five or six good sand/pebble beaches along the coast to the south of the port and across the island. There are other beaches in the north, but they are only accessible by sea.

Livadi offers a sand beach backed by pine trees and a flat strip of insect-ridden marshland. Angale is a long walk from Hora along the ridge of the island, turning left by the windmills; you can often find donkeys at 100 drachmas for the haul back. The best beach on Folegandros is Katergi, a good hour's walk by the inland route via Livadi and across the foothills, or half an hour's boat trip from the port. Katergi has sand on the shore, a strip of pebbles in the water and a small island in the bay, which gives it a beautiful desert island atmosphere. And, it is often deserted. Caiques from Karavostassis harbour charge around 500 drachmas for the round trip, arriving by appointment after a few hours for the return journey.

Karavostassis has two above-average restaurants, including the Remezzo, where Eleni's sophisticated culinary touch can be sampled in a garden seat swinging to the stereophonic strains of Beethoven and an atmosphere more akin to Mykonos than lonely Folegandros.

The main village of Hora is an arid hour's walk uphill, but fortunately there is an orange dormobile providing a bus service four times a day, which turns into a taxi after 7 pm. It makes an evening visit to town a must, and also makes a good case for staying in Hora. The walk downhill to the port and beaches is not painful, the main village is cool and high and there is another village two kilometres along the spine of the island for an easy evening stroll.

Hora itself is a jewel among Cycladic villages with pretty flowered squares and streets, another good restaurant in the square, and terraced vineyards tumbling down a steep hill to the sea. Its discotheque is mercifully outside the village limits on the road to Karavostassis.

A small caique runs between Folegandros, Sikinos and Ios three times a week, taking about an hour between each island. This gives you a chance to catch regular ships of the line running from Milos to Ios and Santorini, though some main ferries do stop at Folegandros and Sikinos.

Travel

BOAT   Up to 4 ferries a week from Piraeus and onward connections to Santorini and Anafi. Weekly ferry to Crete, Rhodes, the Dodecanese and north-east Agean islands. Regular caique service to Sikinos and Ios.

Santorini

One of the most dramatic events in the ancient world has created one of the natural wonders of the modern world at Santorini, an island sometimes called Thira or Kalliste 'the most beautiful'.

A volcanic eruption three or four times the size of Krakatoa gave Santorini its spectacular shape – a sheer crescent of cliffs 1,000 feet high surrounding a lagoon of sea water, once the crater of a high volcano. A volcano which remains active to this day, in small craters in the bay and around the island.

When Santorini blew its top around 1500 BC it landed enough ash and waves on Crete 60 miles away to destroy that island's Minoan cities. It may also have caused the biblical flood and launched the legendary city of Atlantis into the depths of the Aegean. The eruption carpeted the surrounding seabed with black pebbles and pumice stone, created lava islets which emerged from the sea over the next 3,500 years and gave Santorini's beaches their distinctive black sand. It also gave the island vineyards black walls and rich volcanic soil, which produces delicious

grapes and some of the best wines in Greece. Rich reds, sweetish rosés and smokey whites go under names like 'Atlantis' and 'Lava'.

Santorini is the single most spectacular sight in Greece, and so inevitably is on the tourist track. The island has international charter flights, an air link with Athens, regular steamers from Piraeus, Mykonos and Ios, and is a calling point on many Aegean cruises.

Arriving by ship at the island's main port of Kalderas, 1,000 feet below the capital of Thira, can be a unique experience, especially at night, since the traditional link between the two is a steep zig-zag of 587 stone steps two kilometres long. There are islands where you have to take a small boat or bus to the main town, but here the main transport is donkey or mule at about 100 drachmas per sturdy beast. It can be an unnerving trip after dark. A friend of mine ended up riding side-saddle and clinging for dear life to a rampaging mule with his bag tumbling down the steps on one ascent, but it doesn't happen often. Over the past two years the donkey train has been threatened by the arrival of a cable car, which whisks you up the cliff in two minutes flat for the fee of 180 drachmas.

The port of Athinios, has been developed at the southern end of Santorini. This, too, spoils the fun and the enormous incomes of the donkey drivers. But it can still bring tension in the long wait to see whether a bus is going to come to transport the ship's passengers up the winding cliff road to Thira. Athinios is another place to trust in the gods and share a taxi or take the first hotel bus available if it is late at night.

Thira town has some of the world's most scenic accommodation and restaurants, with buildings hanging from the cliff, and a view of ships like toys in a bathtub 1,000 feet blow. But it can be mean and moody, and is a place to be absent from when many cruise ships are calling at once. Then the narrow pebbledash streets are crammed with camera-hung trippers who have only two hours to take the donkey ride, bargain for rugs, have their photos taken and dash back to their ship. This sudden infusion of gullible customers turns the donkey drivers and shopkeepers into mercenary maniacs for a time.

There are regular buses across Santorini, but the best way to see the island is without doubt by motor bike or moped at 600-1,000 drachmas a day. You can then explore the remote black beaches that stretch almost all the way along the east coast, visit half-deserted Oia to witness the force of the last bad eruption in the 1950's and from the sheer cliffs get some idea of the size of the original volcano.

Both sides of Santorini radiate exotic colours, mainly reds, browns, yellows and blacks in layers, which make a strong contrast with green eucalyptus trees along the roads and spotless villages spread like snow across the tips of the cliffs. The whiteness of the island homes is interrupted only by an occasional blue church dome. Almost the whole of the gently sloping east coast is swimmable. The most popular beaches, with regular buses, are Kamari, three-quarters of the way down the island, and Perissa near the tip of the south coast. Both have simple restaurants and Perissa an occasional discotheque.

To get away from the crowds, aim halfway down the island to Monolithos, but be prepared for a dusty road around the airport and a not-so-pretty coastline. There are other deserted coves accessible to moped riders via the coast road that runs north from Thira to Vourvoulos. All the roads run past vineyards where the vines are plaited in circular pig's tails to strengthen them against the wind.

Santorini is now rich in man-made antiquities as well as natural history, thanks to the discoveries in recent years at Akrotiri. There, in a dried-up river bed, a local farm worker noticed the tip of an old building. Subsequent excavations, which are continuing, have revealed a Minoan city buried for 3,500 years under lava. Akrotiri is – thanks to the lava – in a better state of repair than the Minoan cities on

Crete and the excavators are making a better job of reconstruction than Sir Arthur Evans with his ambitious paint and concrete job at Knossos. The tragedy of Akrotiri is that its superb frescoes have been carried away to the Archaeological Museum in Athens for fear of earthquake damage. They portray scenes of sea battles, African expeditions, children boxing, women in varied fashions and exotic flowers, which suggests a more cosmopolitan and less rigid society than that on Minoan Crete. They stir the imagination. No royal palace has been found and the current theory is that Akrotiri was a colony of Knossos, but suppose it was an outpost of a much grander citadel of Atlantis now buried under the sea, with its own African territories sharing in the Pax Minoa?

Akrotiri has its own beach below the site. For those with time, two other sites worth visiting are Ancient Thira and the monastery of Profitis Elias. Ancient Thira is perched on a small plateau above the sea and is mainly Roman with a market, gymnasium, baths and temple of Apollo.

Profitis Elias is a declining monastery, with only two monks in residence. On the highest tip of Santorini, it stands in the shade of a big radar station, but views of the island are impressive and its exhibition of treasures and antiques gives fascinating glimpses of religious and island life a century or two back, including an underground school during the Turkish occupation.

Another pilgrimage worth making on Santorini is by small boat from the port of Thira across to the two black cinder islets that have appeared in the bay in recent centuries. They were smoking with activity as recently as the 1950's. Vegetation is gradually taking root, but the scene around the small craters must be the nearest thing on this planet to the landscape of the moon. You half expect to see a film crew making Star Wars V. The only sign of human activity, sadly, is white paint graffiti plastered over the black rocks of the tiny harbour.

Another islet across the bay is Therassion. This is the place to head for if you need an escape from the excesses of civilisation. It has rooms and restaurants, in its small village, reached by a flight of steps from the port. The harbour beach is pebble, but there is a better one on the other side of the islet.

Travel

FLIGHTS International charter flights. Up to 2 flights daily from Athens (45 mins). One daily flight to Mykonos (40 mins). 3 flights a week to Heraklion on Crete (40 mins). Summer service to Rhodes (40 mins).

BOAT Daily ferries from Piraeus (12 hrs); frequent ferry connections with Crete and Ios, Paxos, Naxos and Milos. Santorini is now also on the major summer cruise routes.

Anafi

The southernmost island of the Cyclades, Anafi is reputed to have risen from the sea at the behest of Apollo to shelter the storm-tossed Argonauts. That is certainly the way it looks to this day and it remains remote and isolated, served only twice a week by ships from Santorini.

Anafi is rocky, with scattered pebble beaches, a small harbour and a monastery. It offers a refuge of peace and quiet to anyone dying to divert from the main tourist routes, even though the natives can be a little stand-offish until you get to know them.

There is one sandy beach with a stream running into it, a short walk from the port. East of the port is a temple of Apollo, and there are also remains of an old castle to the north.

Travel

BOAT Up to 3 ferries a week from Piraeus (13 hrs); 2 ferries a week from Santorini; 1 ferry connection per week with Crete and Rhodes.

Amorgos

It is easy to fall head over heels for Amorgos, once you have survived the long sea journey of 12 hours from Piraeus. East of Naxos and Ios it's a dramatic isle that rises sheer out of the sea and, after Santorini, is the most spectacular of the Cyclades. Amorgos stretches across the sea like an elongated cliff, which swells out at both ends to accommodate fertile terraces and tiered white villages. The two ends are linked only by sea.

The southern harbour of Katapola lies over a deep gulf entered between two awesome cliffs. It has a pebble beach. Six kilometres away, and reached by the only tarmac road, is Chora, the island's main village. To the north of that is the spectacular monastery of Khozoviotissa, which rises direct from the cliff-face over the sea as though built by nature. Today the miraculous icon of Pangia and the dwarflike interior are tended by only three or four monks.

If the south has the holy treasures of Amorgos, the north is more blessed by nature. The charming little port of Aegiali has good footpath links with three other white villages perched on the hilltops behind, and flanking the harbour is a good sandy beach. There are other beaches scattered along the north coast, though you need sturdy walking shoes or a hired boat to visit many of them.

Travel

BOAT Up to 3 ferries a week from Piraeus (12 hrs). Daily summer caique service from Naxos and connections with Santorini, Ios, Astipalea and Kos.

Donoussa, Schinoussa, Keros, Iraklia, Koufonissi

These sparsely inhabited islands lie between Naxos and Amorgos and are occasional calls for ferries that link the two bigger islands.

Schinoussa

Schinoussa has a good harbour at Mersina, lying below a mediaeval castle, and has small island charm, but rooms are hard to come by even in summer.

Iraklia

Iraklia is similar with a pretty little harbour at Iraklia village and a large cave nearby.

Donoussa

Donoussa, an occasional call for ships going from Naxos to Egiali in northern Amorgos, has a prehistoric site across the island from the village.

Keros

Keros is often the last stop for ships steaming on to Katapola on Amorgos. It shows signs of past splendour in the mediaeval castle in the north of the island, but today has only a toy port and a couple of shingle beaches nearby. The name was used by Alastair Maclean for the island where British troops were supposedly marooned by the 'Guns of Navarone'.

Koufonissi

The four sparsely-inhabited islets of Koufonissi are rarely visited by the island steamers, but can be reached by small boat from Schinoussa and Keros.

Koufonissi has some good sandy beaches and one taverna with rooms, which is often limited to fish and egg dishes.

Travel

BOAT   Up to 2 ferries a week from Piraeus to Donoussa, Schinoussa, Iraklia and Keros (over 12 hrs). Infrequent ferries to other islands including Naxos, Amorgos, Santorini and Anafi.

Naxos

Strong historical, mythological and operatic overtones give Naxos an air of mystery and romance. A pretty little port with Venetian castle and tall white houses dotting the hillsides inland add to the fairytale illusion, but, once out of Naxos town, the island is hard put to live up to its image as the most romantic of the Cyclades.

Apparently, Byron fell in love with Naxos on his first visit to Greece and always remembered it as his dream island. But he must have walked the long sandy bay below Naxia before it became a popular camp site and gathering ground for young holidaymakers. However, a walk across the headland and down the west coast is rewarded by a series of long, sandy beaches which are not so crowded. There are rooms to rent at Aghia Anna and Agios Prokopios. Alternatively, take a bus to Pirgaki and walk up the coast, or rent a moped or scooter in the town.

Kastraki is a particularly attractive beach area with sand as far as the eye can see, four restaurants and the remains of an old acropolis.

Two good roads on the main bus routes lead to Apollonia and Apiranthus. Apollonia is an attractive little fishing village with rooms to rent, but its beach is rough, with large pebbles; not a good place to swim when the current is strong. Apiranthus is inland, but a half hour's walk away on the coast are a good shingle beach and rooms at Mutsuna. The road to Apollonia goes past some fertile vineyards which, every autumn, yield a fruity, rough Naxos wine. And a hillside over the village is the eternal resting place of Naxos man – the giant Kouros statue lies supine where it was carved.

Along these roads lie some pretty inland villages. There's Sagri with its fortified monastery; Halki with the ruins of Byzantine churches and a Frankish castle at nearby Epano Kastro; and Filoti which is a short walk from the cave of Zeus on the slopes of towering Mount Zas, and a slightly longer walk from the magnificent sandy curve of Psili Ammos on the east coast. On the road north of Naxos town lies another good stretch of beaches at Akrotiria Amitis.

Turn off the main road before Filoti where a sign says "Kouros", for the Naxos' equivalent of the Garden of Eden where a tiny wizened lady may offer you food from her garden for nothing after you have seen the island's second giant Kouros man.

Naxos town has character, with its narrow streets, whitewashed Cycladic houses and the stately Portada standing like a trademark across the harbour where it once served as the gateway to the temple of Apollo. Nowadays the Portada stands over a more contemporary place of worship labelled 'disco' and 'rock'. There were four discotheques in the port at the last count, but they all hibernate out of season and are safely tucked away over the headland in the bay of Aghios Georgiou. The best eating is to be found by climbing the winding streets off the harbour which contain half a dozen pretty garden restaurants.

Naxos has good sea links with Paros, Mykonos and Ios, plus an occasional ship to Amorgos.

Travel

BOAT   Daily ferries from Piraeus (7 hrs); frequent ferry connections with Paros, Santorini, Ios, Siros and Tinos. Daily tourist boat in summer to Mykonos. Also daily summer caique to Amorgos.

Paros

An island that has started to develop like Mykonos is Paros, fairly and squarely lying in the centre of the Cyclades, and boasting the same cubist houses, windmills and sandy beaches. As it happens, Mykonos was discovered first, but Paros has been catching up by attracting an ever-increasing tourist trade for the past ten years. It has a regular stream of ships from Piraeus, and now has daily flights from Athens.

Gentle hills surround some of the best vineyards in the Cyclades and protect half a dozen coastal villages, which are linked by good roads across and around the island, from the winds that blow across it. Every village seems to have a good long sandy beach including the well-sheltered capital and port of Parikia.

This is a busy town, with whitewashed houses, blue-domed churches, cobbled streets and here and there a hint of the Parian marble that Pericles and his architects selected for the Acropolis in Athens. It has two camp sites and its own beaches curving around the bay, which seem to improve the further around you walk towards the cape that juts out to sea. The furthest beaches are served by boats from the harbour.

Parikia provides good eating from a dozen cafes and restaurants. It also has one of the oldest churches in Greece, the Ekatonta Pyliani, or church of a hundred gates, which was started in the 6th Century AD, though the oldest visible parts date from the Middle Ages. Almost as old is a huge cypress tree growing in the churchyard. This acts as a steeple for the church bells and has proved more durable than the last one which collapsed in an earthquake.

At night you can fondly imagine that the quake was caused by predecessors of a gaggle of bars and discotheques along the sea front, which boom out rock and old Beatles numbers across the waters.

The town straggles along the coast in both directions. It never seems to run back far from the sea, except for the centre, which is a maze of flower-decked white alleyways somewhat reminiscent of the grand maze in Mykonos town. This area contains one of the best restaurants in the Cyclades. It is the oddly named Parostia, which juts into a garden overhung with vines, and serves Paros' own distinguished range of wines, including Lageri, Moulin, Meltemi retsina and red Naoussa. There are two other good restaurants in the main square and one in a garden setting on the

sea front north of the town.

It can be hard to find rooms in high season and the beaches at either end of the town can become crowded, but Paros is an easy island to get around. It has a coastal ring road and there are scooters for hire, plus frequent buses from the windmill on the jetty to a good selection of fine sand beaches and quiet coastal villages, each with their own selection of rooms and small hotels.

This spread of resorts and the preservation of agriculture – corn, cattle and vines – makes Paros feel more like a normal Greek island than a holiday isle blitzed by tourism. It also boasts no less than 17 small satellite isles, many of which have swimmable beaches accessible by boat.

The busiest road across the island is the short, almost walkable, road to Naoussa, a charming miniature fishing harbour of a village, which boasts its own rough red wine, best served chilled.

A good sandy beach runs to the east of the harbour and there are small coves near the odd geometric Hippocampus hotel, but more exotic swimming is across the bay at the other spur of land that protects the village harbour. Naoussa has white winding alleyways decked with tumbling bougainvillea, fashionable bars around the harbour and a first class restaurant in the Christos. It also has a number of modern hotels and some superb beaches within easy walking or scootering distance.

Going east from Naoussa, the nearest beach is the sheltered curve of Lageri where you can swim out to a small island. For variety, walk a little way to the three beaches of Santa Maria, or go as far as Ambelas, which has a separate community with hotel and restaurants in summer. With a car or scooter, it is easy to visit the more remote beaches of Glyfada and Tsoukali. Also Molos, which has two strands, one a superb curve of fine sand enclosed by a large bay and served by three bar/restaurants when they are all functioning. Molos is also within easy walking distance of Piso Livadi, a village of many rooms, a camp site and a good beach across the

headland that supports the monastery of Agios Antonios. An easy walk south from Piso Livadi leads you to the bay of Pounda (second of that name on Paros) and a longish walk brings you to the fabulous curve of Chryssi Akti – literally 'golden beach' or 'gold coast' – which is one of the best in all Greece.

Chryssi Akti has rooms of its own in season and is even nearer to Dryos, a pretty little village of four hotels and many villas strung around a curve of shingle beach backed by cliffs and cane. Dryos and Chryssi Akti are served by the same bus that runs to Marpissa and Piso Livadi.

The road deteriorates between Dryos and Aliki, but there is a rewarding detour to the two shingle beaches of Glyfa. Aliki itself has sprung up fast in recent years and is the third biggest coast resort on Paros.

Although it has a fine curve of sand, plus two good restaurants and the same number of hotels, Aliki somehow lacks the Cycladic charm of Parikia and Naoussa while also missing out on the peaceful, away-from-it-all atmosphere of Dryos and Piso Livadi.

The west coast of the island, opposite Antiparos, has a series of small settlements on the road between Aliki and Pounda, but all are strictly one-horse places, as would be Pounda but for a passable sandy beach, a ferry crossing to Antiparos and a new hotel bravely rising over the beach. There is easy access from the ring road around the coast to the monasteries of Lagovardas, Agios Georgiou, Agios Theodorou, Agios Antonios and Christou Dassous. The road to Christou runs on to Petaloudes, where Paros has tried hard to win its spurs for tourism by creating a Valley of Butterflies similar to the one on Rhodes. Petaloudes is also known locally as Psychopiana and can be reached by donkey from Parikia or by walking up from the coast near Pounda after a bus ride. In a limited summer season it gives the pleasant sight of thousands of mottled red moths rising from the underside of mossy banks and tree trunks along a wet wooded valley.

Ships run daily from Parikia to nearby islands. There are also regular caiques to

Antiparos from Parikia and Pounda – a trip that no-one staying on Paros should miss, if only for a day.

Travel

FLIGHTS Up to 2 flights daily from Athens (55 mins).

BOAT Up to 20 ferries a week from Piraeus (6 hr 30 mins); up to 2 ferries a day to Naxos and frequent ferry connections with Crete, Mykonos, Ios, Kos, Rhodes, Santorini and Siros. Daily caique service to Antiparos.

Antiparos

Clinging close to its west coast, Antiparos is the biggest of the 17 satellite islands of Paros. It has an appealing little village with six busy restaurants and the same number of small hotels along the side of a lagoon-like harbour.

Antiparos rivals Paros for sandy beaches and they are closer together, half a dozen within easy walking distance of the port. The curved beaches backed by pines and scrub, give Antiparos, as much as any island in Greece, a desert island atmosphere. That is true even though there are three or four boats a day from Parikia and Pounda, and the port now has rooms for 2,000 visitors, and half a dozen bars and discotheques.

Boats also run along the coast facing Paros to a small beach from which a rough track runs uphill about two kilometres to a long sloping cave festooned with stalactites and stalagmites. It is a hard walk uphill on a hot day followed by a long descent by steps to the cave, but the journey is made easier by a donkey man who stands on the beach every day in summer, and a little cafe by the sea which serves soft drinks and simple food of the tomato, omelette and grapes variety. You can go to the opposite extreme and walk all the way from Antiparos, but it is a hard two hours slog on a hot day and it pays to take the boat one way at 80 drachmas.

Whether on foot or boat, the journey does open up some of the wonders of Antiparos. It has three good curves of sand just south of the port, within easy walking distance, plus one across the headland from the port and a long stretch of dune beach to the north between Antiparos and Kato Fira where there is a camp site. There are plenty of other remote swimmable coves just off the single road that runs south along the coast and others across the southern headland at Agios Georgios, which are sometimes visited by boat in summer. Kato Fira has yet more remote beaches reached by boat from the port.

Mykonos

Mykonos is fashionable, cosmopolitan and touristy. It dances the night away and sleeps late. There is nudism on many beaches, notably the Paradise and the Super Paradise complex, where the police turn a blind eye to mass body worship. There is also a homosexual community.

Surprisingly, Mykonos was little more than a stopover en route for the wonders of Delos until the 1950's. Even in the early 60's it was a simple Greek island with a good line in whitewashed cubist houses, windmills and 365 churches. It had its own rough red wine and a pelican called Peter.

Nowadays it is internationally renowned, and agriculture has almost ceased in favour of tourism. Cruise ships call daily and a rich horseshoe of narrow streets through the town, as well as the waterfront, is lined with good, but often expensive, restaurants, bars and boutiques, selling fur coats, fashion clothes, jewellery and Greek handicrafts. They are the landmarks on any walk through the maze of streets, where it is easy to get lost, even after a week. You can eat well on a Greek cuisine spiced with international dishes, in restaurants like 'The Waves' beneath the windmills or the fish restaurants along Mykonos' own 'Little Venice' harbour. You can also live well, with hot showers and sunny balconies in the dozen small hotels that have sprung up in the past twenty years.

But there is a sad side to it. Tourism swells the population of Mykonos ten times over in summer and there are bad pressure points. The banks, buses and some of the beaches are unnecessarily crowded as though the islanders are trying to pinch every last penny from their guests. Service can be slow and bar prices ridiculously high. The landladies who meet the boats and planes often overcharge for their simple rooms around the harbour; it is better to look independently for accommodation. And the restaurants like to sell expensive wines. "Mykonos has no wine and we have no small bottles of retsina", is the standard response of restauranteurs, delivered in perfect English.

In spite of all this, Mykonos has great charm. It has learned to live with mass tourism better than some Greek islands and is not festooned with high-rise hotels. It is incredibly pretty, with nearly 400 wedding cake churches and many more dovecotes dotting its barren brown landscape. It has a casual, but sophisticated, nightlife, which at its best is worth the money. The frenzied, silvered dance floor at Piero's Bar justifies a premium on drink prices. So does the musical serenity of Kastro's where you can sit above the sea and study the reflections of the moon or lights from the old town, while sipping one of the incomparable Kastro coffees – a variant of Irish coffee. The island has no antiquities of its own, but does have regular trips to the Sacred Isle of Delos, and a charming little folklore museum behind the Tourist police station for rainy days.

Most days on Mykonos are white hot and the island is not lacking for those occasions. There are welcoming sandy beaches on the north, south and west coasts, reached by regular buses, motor bikes or small boats from the harbour.

Venture beyond the beach to the left of town, and don't stick slavishly to the

Paradise complex. You can find almost deserted beaches at Elia, Anna Bay, Kalafatis and the big bay of Panormos and Ftelia, which can all be reached by bus via the monastery of Ano Mera. Kalafatis also has a large package tour hotel, which charges highly for indifferent food. Within half and hour's walk of the town, there are other good strands at Ornos, San Stefano, Korfos and Agios Ioannis. The coast along to Agios Stefanos has two sizeable hotels.

It is as silly to ignore the Plati Yialos-Paradise beach complex as to try no other. After swaying across the island in the intimate company of 65 others in a bus meant to carry 25, you have a choice of six sandy coves, of which four are far more crowded than others. Most have coarse sand. The best sand and eating is on Psarou to the right of the bus stop. Plati Yialos has a choice of restaurants, the bus stop, and two hotels of its own. Paradise can be reached by walking or boat from Plati Yialos, as can Super Paradise – which is a fairly hard walk – and is more nude and camp than its more accessible neighbour. Many of the couples decorating the sand are slender young men with a taste for bright colours and jewellery. The boats sometimes go on to Elia beach. Since two equally good sandy coves between Plati Yialos and Paradise are simultaneously bare of people, it is tempting to conclude that Paradise is closer to the spirit of Narcissus than that of Apollo.

Mykonos is often windy. More so, it seems than any other Greek island, which may be explained by its lack of high ground and its position near the vortex of the Cycladic wind system. So it pays to check on the direction of the prevailing wind and plan your beach accordingly. The island has regular planes from Athens and ships from Piraeus. But, don't bank everything on one ship, especially in July-August when the meltemmi blows hard in the central Aegean.

There are hotels flanking most of the main beaches around Mykonos and there is a clear case for staying out of town in high season if you are keener to have the pick of places on the beaches than to trip the light fantastic every evening. But be warned, the hotels on Elia and Agios Stefano beaches can be expensive, even for an omelette or coffee, let alone a week's full board.

The best choice for out-of-towners must be Plati Yialos, where you have a choice of hotels and restaurants and a road to town that is just walkable, and affordable by taxi, when the buses stop running in the evening.

Travel

FLIGHTS   International charter flights. Up to 5 flights a day from Athens (50 mins). 3 flights a week from Rhodes (50 mins). 3 flights a week from Santorini (40 mins).

BOAT   Up to 3 ferries a day from Piraeus (6-8 hrs); daily ferries from Rafina. Good connections with other Cyclades islands and Rhodes and Kos. Daily boats to Delos.

Delos

A terrace of lions – or to be more exact lionesses – has become the modern symbol of Delos, the sacred isle of Apollo, up to an hour away by caique from Mykonos harbour. The lions could have been sculpted by a modern artist and seem to forge a link between the present and the ancient past of an island, which is one of the most complete and impressive archaeological sites in Greece.

Legend says that Delos wandered beneath the waves until Poseidon raised it out of the sea on diamond pillars to be the birthplace of Apollo and his sister Artemis. That was enough to launch the island as a sacred sanctuary, where it was forbidden for anyone to be born or die. This law seems to have been respected for centuries, with sudden birth pangs or heart attacks winning a swift passage to the nearby isle of Rhinia, or Great Delos, which guards Delos to the west as Mykonos does to the east. The tiny rocky isle of Delos, with

nothing but its reputation to commend it, became the treasury of the Athenian empire in its golden age and the commercial centre of the Aegean. But after that it was frozen in time, invaded only by nature. No-one lived on the island until recent years, so there was no disturbance of the layout of the ancient city, which covers a large portion of the island and offers a galaxy of delights to modern visitors.

There are four impressive temples, the Sacred Way, the Lion's Way, stadium, gymnasium, shops and the treasury, the last seeming to get less attention than it deserves. Many visitors are diverted by a curious collection of brothels in the midst of the town that almost rank in size and splendour with those at Pompei. These and a row of giant phalluses, now sadly broken, but which once pointed grandly at the sun are probably wed more to Apollo worship than the sexual ceremonies that went on in the brothels.

Let your imagination run in the House of the Trident; the House of the Dolphin and the House of Cleopatra. The superb mosaics should help, especially the magnificent one of Dionysus. If a modern Herodotus compiled seven wonders of the ancient world from those surviving to this day, Delos would have to be one of them.

Delos was pillaged of most of its treasures by waves of pirates and invaders over twenty centuries and its permanent population nowadays are lizards and archaeologists, but it gets a good crowd of visitors almost every day of the year from cruise ships and nearby Mykonos. Caiques go over from Mykonos harbour most mornings, returning early in the afternoon.

Travel

BOAT   Daily service from Mykonos during summer months (30 mins).

There's an informality about
the country that you find
nowhere else in Europe.

PAROS
Blue dom
Parikia,

urches dominate
capital.

'Little Venice' on Mykonos is
a great place to eat fish
and watch the sunset.

TINOS

Votive offerings on sale at the cathedral in Tinos. The icon of the Virgin here is believed to have curative powers.

HALKIDIKI

Halkidiki - lovely, almost
unchangeable countryside
and long, curving beaches.

Siros

All the island steamer routes across the central Aegean meet at Siros, the capital and main commercial centre of the Cyclades. Many people see something of the island en route for Paros, Mykonos, Ikaria, Tinos or even Chios, but most of those that stop off to stay awhile are Greeks.

It is understandable, because the main port of Ermoupolis is big, busy and lacking in the obvious charm of many island harbours. Yet it is a fascinating place for an overnight stay between islands and can make a good base for visiting other islands on day boat trips without the hassle of returning to Piraeus. Nor is the island lacking in character or beaches if you are prepared to explore with the help of its busy network of bus services.

Ermoupolis itself is an impressive sight, rising like an amphitheatre of colour over the harbour with each high point capped by a stately red-roofed church. A closer inspection suggests two or three pyramids of white cubes superimposed on each other, with Ano Siros rising above the harbour of Ermoupolis. The effect comes from stepped streets of white and colour-washed mansions. This was the main port of Greece in the 19th Century and the evidence is still there in big wharves along the harbour and pretty squares behind, spilling over with cafes, kebab stalls and bouganvillea. It is a cheap town to stay and eat in, and has a quota of cinemas, plus regular ships to Tinos, Paros and Mykonos.

There is a friendly little pebble beach in a sheltered cove just north of the town, but for a day on the beach it is worth a half-hour bus trip to Posidonia, Megalo Yialos, Vari, Kinio or Finikas, which all boast sandy strands and places to stay. Better, remote beaches can be found by walking north of Kinio and beyond Galissas on the same coast.

Siros shares the Catholic faith with Tinos and there are many little churches in Ano Siros, but the island does not have the shrine-like atmosphere of its northern neighbour, despite the grand way the Catholic cathedral stands on one high point of the town and the Orthodox cathedral on another, as if each faith is flaunting the other in full view of passing travellers.

Travel

BOAT   Up to 3 ferries a day from Piraeus (4 hrs 30 mins); daily ferry from Rafina via Andros and Tinos.
Frequent and regular ferry connections to the rest of the Cyclades islands.

Tinos

Take the island steamer on from Andros and you pass some weird, wild cliffs which could pass for Scylla and Charibidis, the clashing rocks of the ancient world. The island beyond the rocks is Tinos, the 'Lourdes of Greece', where the Orthodox church bows to Catholicism and an island saint is replaced by the Virgin Mary.

Her white marble church, Panagia Evangelistria, dominates the town and harbour. Twenty years ago, when the daily ships to Mykonos called at Tinos, they used to empty their Greek passengers by the hundreds to surge from the quayside up the wide main street to the holy place, leaving the boat almost deserted except for a handful of tourists wondering whether they were going to the right island.

Near the cathedral are seats and arcades where pilgrims and sick people gather for a blessing from the miraculous jewelled icon of the Virgin, which is believed to have curative powers. The walls are hung with tiny silver offerings shaped like legs, arms or other parts the sick want cured.

Regular buses run the length of the island to Panormos in the north where there is a passable beach. There is another to the west of the town flanking the Tinos Beach Hotel. But the beaches of Tinos do not stand comparison with those of any of its neighbours – Andros, Mykonos and Siros.

More distinguished are its churches – well over 1,000 – and its 600 dovecotes, similar to those on Mykonos. It is unquestionably a pretty island with blue and white buildings rising from a brown landscape and occasional outcrops of greenery.

Tinos was borne as a shrine of the Catholic church in 1822 during the War of Independence against the Turks when, the story goes, the Virgin appeared before an 80 year old nun and told her that a precious icon was buried in a field. The islanders searched and found the jewelled icon. Later they built the Shrine of the Anunciation over the spot.

In more recent years, so another story goes, the islanders of Tinos performed a most irreligious act with Peter, the Mykonos pelican, when he flew over for a visit. They clipped his wings, so that he would stay on Tinos. A fleet of caiques set sail from Mykonos to do battle for their pelican, but he was rescued by the Prime Minister telegraphing Tinos ordering the release of the 'sacred' bird.

Travel

BOAT   Daily ferries from Piraeus (5 hrs 30 mins) and Rafina via Andros. Daily ferries to Mykonos and Siros; also twice-weekly connections with Rhodes.

Andros

If you don't fancy a long sea voyage to an Aegean island, and want sandy beaches combined with a modicum of civilisation, Andros offers an easy solution. It lies only three hours away from the port of Rafina on the east coast of Attica, which in turn is a pleasant one to one-and-half hours' bus journey from Athens through the Attic wine country.

As well as being one of the two most accessible islands by boat – the other is Kea – Andros is one of the biggest islands in the Aegean and certainly the most fertile of the Cyclades. It offers the unusual sight of neatly terraced hillsides, cypress and olive groves and green meadows, with grazing cattle, stretching down to the sea. Yet it is not as much visited by tourists as some of the burnt brown central Aegean islands.

Gavrion and Batsi, only eight kilometres apart, are the charming twin harbours on the west side of the island and have most of the beaches, the restaurants and the nightlife – including three discotheques between them.

Gavrion is the ferry port, linked to Rafina, but that need not be a limiting factor since buses meet the ferries and go to Batsi as well as Andros and Korthion, the two main towns on the east side of the island. The port's big plus points are that it has scooters for hire at 800 drachmas a day, and it is surrounded by sandy coves, three in the bay itself and another four or five along the road to Batsi.

The longest, sometimes called Chryssi Ammos ('golden beach'), is the best sand beach on the island and is only a half hour's walk from the port. Clearly earmarked for building developments, it boasts an above average beach taverna, run by a character called Little John by some British patrons. If you find Chryssi Ammos too crowded, just walk over the headland towards Batsi where there is another good strand, usually less populated.

It is easy to understand why Batsi has taken off as the major resort in the past ten years. A fishing harbour with successive tiers of white red-roofed houses, this is the most picturesque village on the island. Batsi also offers ample accommodation in all grades from simple rooms to small hotels and there is good eating from a choice of seven restaurants and a modicum of nightlife with a thriving cinema and the liveliest discotheque of the trio along this coast.

Batsi is quieter than Gavrion, is on the main bus route and has a good quota of beaches, two inside the curve of the harbour and three on its south side. The harbour bay has the best sand, but dedicated sun-worshippers can also walk along the cliffs to a sandy beach and taverna half an hour south of the village. A pleasant walk inland leads to the monastery of Zoodos Pigi ('spring of life') and the village of Kato Katakoilos.

Paleopolis, a short bus ride or longish walk

south of Batsi, is a charming old village with a thousand steps down to a long pebble beach. Alas, there is no taverna on the beach, but local legend says that the old capital of Andros is buried under the sea nearby.

The modern capital, which is called Andros or Hora, stands proud on a headland with a good sandy beach on both sides. It is a grand town on the east coast with tall mansions and a paved pedestrian walkway. This leads to a small tree-lined square where you can take coffee with views over the sea and a small tower standing on a rock off the headland, destined for photographs and picture postcards.

Andros town is worth staying in for a while; it has the island's only reliable bus service and is within easy distance of Apikia, which has the monastery of Marinas and produces the famous mineral water. From the town, it's not far to walk to Stenies, below which are the two superb sand beaches of Yialia, one with a friendly taverna and the other with a desert island atmosphere. A long walk, or donkey ride away, is the island's most splendid monastery, Panachrantou, suspended from the side of Mount Gerakonas. It is rich in icons.

Those who seek somewhere quieter should make the bus journey along the high cliffs of the west coast, and inland through a spectacular valley of villages and fertile fields to Korthion, which lies south of Andros town. Here rooms and restaurants can be found along the alleys that lead from its straggling main street, and the beach south of the village is prime sand.

Andros makes its own wine, usually resinated, and has other local specialities in its pastry shops. It makes a good first stop on a tour of the northern Cyclades because in summer it has frequent ferry connections, which run along the west side of the island on a two-hour trip to Tinos, and on to Siros, Mykonos and Paros.

Travel

BOAT	2/3 ferries a day from Rafina (3 hrs); daily ferries to Tinos and connections to Mykonos and Siros.

Athens

Athens must be leading contender for the title of the ugliest capital in Europe, as well as the hottest, dustiest and noisiest. Yet the city contains places of great charm and beauty. The ladylike Acropolis, sophisticated Syntagma Square and the peerless archaeological museum must wince at the cacophony of horns, squealing tyres and shouts of the street-barkers, if not at the rubbish-strewn side streets, the tread of a million camera-hung tourists and the semi-permanent pall of pollution that overhangs Pericles' long walls to Piraeus. But they go on living side by side, making Athens a place of pilgrimage with something of the holy atmosphere that transcends the trivia of other hotspots like Jerusalem, Istanbul and Alexandria.

Geography and the spirit of the 5th Century BC, rather than the long march of history, have made it the capital of Greece. Athens was a supreme military power for only half a century. After 404 BC, it played slave to many masters; Sparta, Macedonia, Rome, the Franks, the Venetians and the Turks. Other cities were called capital of Greece – Corinth, Salonika and Naufplion among them – but in the end Athens was the natural choice for the independent Greece that emerged in 1830. It has been capital since 1834. A point worth remembering, though, is that Athens was only a small town until the 1920's when over a million Greeks were expelled from Turkey and set up in the jerry-built suburbs that now stretch all the way down to Piraeus. The carefully planned new town was transformed overnight into a sprawling concrete jungle.

And yet nothing touched the heart of the city, and it beats proudly still on the hills of the Acropolis, the Pnyx and the Lycabettus. All roads in Athens seem to lead up to the Acropolis, as well they might. If there were a new classification today of the Wonders of the Ancient World, it would take its place at once beside the Pyramids. Sparkling white by day, and gleaming gold by night when the surrounding spotlights do their work, and sound and light displays are given, it is a massive marble memorial to the Golden Age of Greece of the 5th Century BC.

The spirit of the age still shines through the four temples of the rock – the Propylaea, the temple of Wingless Victory, the Erechtheion and the regal Parthenon. Although designed by different architects, they have a collective shape and unity. Art and science and mystery unite too in the way the columns are spaced at irregular intervals and are tapered, so that at almost any vantage point they look regularly spaced and absolutely straight. It is a shame that you have to visit the museum of the Acropolis and the British Museum in London to see more detailed decorative work of the four temples, but it is remarkable enough that so much remains after centuries of neglect, Turkish gunpowder, and modern pollution.

Beneath the rock of the Acropolis lie other wonders of the Ancient World; the theatre of Dionysos and the Odeon of Herod Atticus. Opposite, stands the Areopagus hill, with only a few traces of when it made and kept the laws of ancient Athens. Here, too, is the Pnyx, where orators like Demosthenes warned the Athenians against Philip, and Socrates took the hemlock. This is now used as an auditorium for sound and light displays.

On the opposite side of the hill, lower down, stand the ancient market, the arcade of Attalus and the amazingly well-preserved temple of Hephaistos, usually known as the Theseion. Walk around the third part of this circle of wonders and you will find the monument of Lysicrates, Hadrian's triumphal arch and the appropriately tall pillars of Olympian Zeus.

See all this and die, the poet might have said. But it is essential to stay alive – even in the toiling mid-summer heat of Athens – long enough to visit the Archaeological Museum out along Patission, via Omonia Square. There you are not overwhelmed by sheer size, as in the British Museum, or some of the Italian art galleries, but by seeing face to face so many statues and works of art that have previously been postcards or illustrations in books. It is worth coming just to see the massive bronze of Poseidon, hauled from the sea off Sounion. Or is it Zeus minus his lightning? Then there's the golden death mask of Agamemnon – or could it be his murderer Aegisthus? The happy Kouroi – what do they find so pleasing? Look for the crouching jockey – or was he really a 'Boy on a Dolphin', dreamed up for the book and film of the same name? These mysteries are surrounded by rooms crammed full of pottery, statues, weapons, armour and jewellery. Enough to complete and complement a day that started on the Acropolis and its surroundings, and leave sufficient energy to see something of Byzantine Athens and the modern city.

The Byzantine and Benaki museums, both on Vassilissis Sofias Avenue, house magnificent collections of Byzantine art, ikons, frescoes, gold ornaments and ecclesiastical ornaments. Combine them with visits to the 11th Century church of Agios Apostoli, the 12th Century Agios Eleftherios or the 11th Century Agios Theodori and Kapnikarea.

Modern Athens starts in the stately squares of Syntagma and Omonia, connected by the twin one-way streets of Stadiou and Venizelou. The rich and the curious sip coffee in the outdoor cafes of Syntagma, or scan the fashion and jewellery shops of Stadiou, while the poor make for the snack bars that cram the narrow alleys around Omonia. The tourist walks on past the Grande Bretagne and King George Hotels to look at the Parliament building –

guarded by evzones in their curious dolly dresses and slippers – the National Park Garden and the hill of the Lycabettus with its funicular railway and view of the City. Or they make for the 'flea market' off Monastiraki where anything from antiques and handicrafts to sturdy sandals and ripe melons can be bought.

If you seek patterned rugs, sandals or tourist souvenirs, the best bargain will probably be found along Pandrossou. If you want a fur or leather coat, try nearby Ermou or Metropoleos. If your needs go no further than an English newspaper, a bar of chocolate, a postcard or a phone call, they can all be bought at the little kiosks that surround the main square and line the main streets.

For eating out in the evening try the grill houses around Omonia Square where lambs, chickens and suckling pigs roast slowly on rotating spits. One evening will have to be set aside for a visit to the Plaka, the old quarter of Athens, around the Acropolis, which is crammed with late-night restaurants, bars and nightclubs. Guided tours often include an evening visit to this area. But be warned, restaurants are not cheap and can charge fancy prices for drinks accompanied by dance music or live entertainment. The Plaka sells its atmosphere at a premium.

Over three-quarters of all people going to Greece for the first time go to Athens. Apart from its native charm, the city is the obvious transit stop for virtually the whole country. It has the buses, the railway, the largest airport and the port of Piraeus. The last is reached either by bus from the centre of Athens or by the swift, if uncomfortable, underground railway that runs through Omonia and Monastiraki.

But most of those who stay in the city feel an urge to get out of it after a few days of doing the sites. They often ask – what else is there to do after seeing the obvious sites – the Acropolis, the market, the museums and the churches? Where else to go? The same questions are asked by those who reluctantly spend a day in Athens at the beginning or end of their holiday to play safe and fit the schedules of island ships to those of airlines.

The most obvious trip out of the city is to the seaside along the south coast of Attica – the coastal road that Anthony Perkins took with suicide on his mind and the strains of Bach on his car radio in the film 'Phaedra'. It goes under the romantic name of the 'Athenian Riviera' and boasts a string of resorts with names like Voula, Glyfada, Vouliagmeni and Lagonissi. These can look fabulous in tourist leaflets, but alas are not as good as they seem or sound, and the Riviera has its suicidal aspects along with its sunshine. It is a busy coast road which can be hell to cross. The restaurants and cafes are expensive and sometimes it is hard to get served. The beaches are crowded and usually demand an entry fee. The water is often polluted. And, worst of all, most of this coast is the approach path to Athens international airport, which sees a plane in and out every two minutes. All this makes the 'Athenian Riviera' one of the most unlovely coasts in Greece.

It is still worth taking a bus as far as Cape Sounion, 70 kilometres distance from Athens, to see the lovely little temple of Poseidon perched on its promontory and to swim off one of the sandy beaches close by. It is also well worth taking a bus across the Attica peninsula, through its wine country, to the honest little seaside resorts and beaches on the east coast like Nea Makri, Rafina, Porto Rafti, Loutsa, Paralia, Marathona, Lavrion and Agia Marina. Try the coast road to Sounion and the country route back.

Most of the resorts of the east coast can be reached within a maximum of an hour and a half, about the same time it takes to reach the Riviera resorts. Sometimes a day trip can take in a ship to Evia, Kea or Andros, and there are other interests besides swimming on the coast. There's the battlefield of Marathon, where a tiny Athenian army saw its finest hour running down the Persian hordes as they embarked from their ships, Vravrona with the temple of Artemis and Ramnous with its temple of Nemesis.

West of Athens are seaside resorts with good, if pebble, beaches at Kineta, Loutraki and Porto Germeno. There is also Elefsis, (or Eleusis) with its sanctuary of mysteries, and Dafni, which has an 11th Century monastery and summer wine festivals. Finally, there are the islands of the Saronic Gulf. Aegina is only a thirty-five minutes ride by Hydrofoil away from Piraeus. A pleasant, quiet place to spend an involuntary overnight stop waiting for a plane from Athens next day.

Central Greece

This is a land of mountains, lakes and rivers, and some surprisingly big towns. It is a land that can be both wild and mysterious. No wonder the Ancient Greeks sited their oracles in these echoing hills and accredited the biggest of all, Mount Olympus, with the seat of the Gods. When the tips of the mountains are cloaked in cloud, you can see them still ruling and protecting all they survey. Something to think about when winter skiing at the tiny resort on Olympus.

The road network in central Greece is one of the best in the country, but beware of reading or trying to write postcards when travelling by bus. The roads wind and wriggle like snakes, twisting the intestines at every turn. There is plenty to see on and around the roads. Apart from spectacular scenery, you can spot some exotic wildlife; giant tortoises, birds of prey and storks, which rest on the steeples of churches as if they know they are on protected ground. If the fur shops are any guide, there are wolves here and there too. Everything is larger than life. On a scooter trip across Epirus from Corfu, I was surprised to feel the shadow of a small plane across my tiny vehicle. But I was not prepared to see a hungry-looking fish eagle with red beak and black and white markings, at least six-foot across the wings. He must have taken the scooter for a sheep in fourth gear and showed no fear as he landed on the road 20 yards away. There he stayed until thankfully an oncoming Metaxa lorry hooted him back into the air.

The first port on the west coast of central Greece is Igoumenitsa, a major ferry link with Italy and Corfu. Despite its role as a port, it is a delightful little seaside town with a long curving beach. Not at all a bad place to be marooned in for a few hours or overnight while waiting for a ferry or bus connection.

If you take the coast road south from Igoumenitsa, you soon hit the seaside resort of Parga, the jewel of western Greece. It has three sandy beaches on separate bays fringed by islands. Above each bay stands a castle, and Parga looks more like an island port than a mainland resort. It is a good place to linger in on this coast and the advent of tourism has brought good restaurants, wind surfing, discotheques and daily excursions to the isle of Paxos and to Necromanteion, the mythical entrance to the underworld.

Further south the road forks inland for Arta, a pretty town boasting a 13th Century castle and church to match, and south for Preveza, the main port of Epirus with a ferry link across the straits and a right turn for the island of Lefkas, linked to the mainland by a narrow road along a causeway.

Messolonghi, on the mouth of the gulf of Patras, has a special place in modern Greek history, for its heroic role in the 19th Century War of Independence. Here the English poet, Byron, came with funds and new hope during a four-year siege. He died for the cause – from fever – and his statue stands proud in modern Messolonghi. The town is now approached over a lagoon, which serves as a fish hatchery and attracts storks to the town's rooftops. In every way this stretch of water gives Messolonghi character it might not otherwise have.

A prettier town in itself is Nafpaktos, on the north side of the Gulf of Corinth. It rises white from the blue sea with a harbour guarded by two Venetian towers and with passable stony beaches.

Halfway along the north shore of the Gulf lies the port of Itea, which can also be reached by ferry from the Peloponnese, by far the least painful route for visitors to Delphi. The alternative is a long winding bus or car journey from Athens, but with the compensation of some spectacular scenery on the way.

Visit Delphi and seek your future in the vale of the most revered oracle. It will grant you a vision more precious than that offered by any modern fortune tellers and without having to cross its palm with silver. You are joining an exclusive and ancient club of which Oedipus was a founder member.

Delphi is set in a grassy amphitheatre looking down on white Itea, green olive groves and the blue Gulf. Hotel-keepers and restauranteurs have taken advantage of the view in siting their establishments along the main street of the town. This swings with dance music through the summer and the winter as well, when Delphi is used as base camp for skiers on Parnassus, Greece's premier ski resort. It is a brave try at a ski centre, but until far more lifts are added, it will make a poor comparison with the run of other international resorts.

But, Delphi itself needs no gimmicks. The sanctuary of Apollo houses his temple, the Sacred Way, stadium, theatre and museum as well as the Castalian Spring, from which both pilgrims and oracle drank in ancient times. From Delphi it is a relatively short way to the isolated Byzantine monastery of Ossios Loukas. Here, two interconnecting churches are surmounted by a large dome and house some superb mosaics as well as icons.

Back to Igoumenitsa, the other main road goes eastwards to Ioannina. Approached from the other direction or the air, this smart, bustling town can be seen at its best, reflected in the lake with its island in the foreground. The castle promontory of the self-seeking Turkish governor, Ali Pasha, looks like a second island. There is now a restaurant on the island and many more along the shore, where they serve frogs legs and eels and trout from the lake. You can wash these all down with sparkling Zitsa wine – the not-so-bad Greek answer to champagne. If you visit Zitsa itself, a few kilometres away, you will be treading in the footsteps of Byron, but don't expect a shrine or posh cafes. Zitsa is a modest little hill village much like any other, except for its explosive local drink served in containers that look much like coke bottles with a cork.

A little further away to the south is Dodoni, site of the oldest oracle and best amphitheatre in Greece. Its magical setting is well worth a visit if you are in this area. Metsovon is a neat red-roofed town, typical of the area. Others like Trigona and Panagia bear witness to recent earthquakes with their corrugated roofs. All slot into the hillsides like a geometric pattern. Above and beyond, the mountains are adorned with cool fir, plane, beech and oak trees and lush grasslands on which herds of sheep and horses graze. When autumn tints the deciduous foliage, this whole area resembles the English Lake District or the north Italian Alps; an illusion that's changed by the appearance of decidedly Greek-looking goatherds, with their crooks and baggy pants.

You can see the stubby grey peaks of Meteora from ten miles away. These are the Dolomites of Greece. Perched on their crests are more than thirty monasteries, four of them inhabited, and all defying gravity and the conventions of architecture. Stay in Kalambaka or Kastrika and take the early morning bus to the foot of the Great Meteoro built around 1360, separated by an awesome gulf, but only five minutes walk over bridges, from the Varlaam Monastery. Original entry was by basket only, or ladder up the steep cliffs. Now there are easy stone steps, but heavy items like building materials are still hauled up in basket lifts reinforced nowadays with steel rope. The monastery chapels are plastered with frescoes of the saints and martyrs, dying in some cases in more ingenious ways than their tormentors could have devised at the time. The big monasteries boast museums with early parchment bibles, golden icons and religious vestments. Great Meteoro also has a grisly memento of the monks who have toiled for centuries to make these beautiful things – a room full of skulls lit only by a candle.

Women are allowed into the Meteora monasteries, but only in long skirts, not in trousers. The holy atmosphere is spoiled a bit, though, by endless notices, entry fees to each sanctuary and tourist shops prominently displayed inside the holy places. The rock chimneys of Meteora reflect the early sun with a pink glow around their peaks and might have been tailor-made by God for monastic communities to worship Him in grand isolation, smack in the middle of mainland Greece. They have also supplied this remote region with a tourist trade it would not otherwise enjoy.

Beyond Meteora and Trikala, the next big town up the valley, the mountains give way to flat plains on which cotton, corn and eucalyptus trees grow, signalling that you are approaching the fertile flatlands of Macedonia. The east coast from Volos to Thessalonika has some good sandy beaches and camp sites along the coastal plain, backed and protected by the steep wooded hillsides of Mounts Pelion, Ossa and Olympus. But it is not the most exciting coastline in Greece. There are greater prizes beyond Thessalonika.

The Far North
The mountainous far north of Greece, west of Salonica, is an area few tourists penetrate by choice, though some encounter it when coming into Greece from Yugoslavia. The most spectacular town of the area, and the most colourful to stay in, is the fur-making centre of Kastoria, built on a peninsula bounded on two sides by a lake, which the locals fish from oblong punts. The lake is lined by tall houses with wooden bays projecting over the water.

The feeling of 'Alpine Greece' becomes more acute around Florina, Veria, Naoussa and Edessa where rivers plunge down from the hills into lakes, and nearby Seli and Vigla offer modest skiing when snow caps Mount Vermioz and Verno in the winter.

Campers or motorists staying along the coast between Platamonas and Paralia must be tempted to try to climb Mount Olympus and commune with some of the world's most ancient gods. They should be warned that the peak is 9,500 feet above sea level, is permanently snow-capped and the last 2,000 feet is strictly for rock climbers with ropes and ice-picks. You can, however, climb 3,600 feet up by car, driving along a winding road via Litochoro and the Dionysius monastery – called after the Athenian friend of St Paul, not the god – to a spectacular little camp site and cafe, where the mountains provide shelter from the winds and there are mules for hire for the next stage of the ascent. That goes up a rough path nearly 4,000 feet to an Alpine Federation hostel, bookable from Litochoro for about 200 drachmas a night. This site sits proudly at the base of Zeus' throne, a huge curved basin of scree stretching up to the celestial summit. It is a hard climb, but the views and atmosphere are ample reward. The whole journey can be made by the fit in a day from the coast.

Travel

FLIGHTS	1 daily flight from Athens to Ioannina (55 mins). 4 flights a week from Athens to Kastoria (1 hr 30 mins). 3 flights a week from Athens to Kozani (1 hr 5 mins).
ROAD	There is a good bus service from Athens to main parts of Central Greece.
TRAINS	Daily trains from Athens to Larissa, Volos, Trikala and Kozani.

North Eastern Greece

The area fanning out eastwards from Thessalonika to the Turkish border is almost Greece in miniature. It has its own three-pronged Peloponnese in Halkidiki, big coastal ports like Kavala and Alexandroupolis and close connections to three islands – Thassos, Samothraki and Lemnos.

The city dominating this area, and the second biggest in Greece, is the bustling, sophisticated port and university centre of Thessalonika. It is a fast, confusing city to arrive in as a stranger – more so than Athens – and remains remote and slightly mysterious when you get to know it better. Why, for instance, are there so few open air restaurants? Why are many of its historical treasures so often closed to the public? Why are there so few fishing boats in the Gulf of Thermaikos? Could it be partly climate, partly history? Thessalonika, or Salonica, or Thessaloniki, was named after the half-sister of Alexander the Great, the boy king of Macedonia who conquered as far as India. Still the capital of Macedonian Greece to this day, it is Athens and Piraeus rolled into one, but with a climate more temperate than that of Attica and island Greece.

Thessalonika has a proud historical past, but what remains is not of the period of Alexander, who left his cultural bequest elsewhere. The city's finest historical monuments are Roman; the Arch of Galerius resplendent with cavalry, elephants and chariots; the mausoleum; the baths, theatre, market and Exedra; the walls to the north of the town, giving proof of what good cement those ingenious people used. All this reflects Thessalonika's importance as a link between the capitals of the eastern and western empires, Byzantium and Rome.

The modern city pivots on the 15th Century Venetian white tower and the modern black statue of Alexander on his horse. From there a rich residential area runs along the eastern seaboard behind a strip of parkland. To the west lie the harbour, railway station, open green squares and hotels. It is usually easy to find a room in Thessalonika, but beware the Ides of September when the city's famous trade fair takes place and thousands of free-spending salesmen flood the hotels with business.

The trade fair ground occupies the hinge of the city above the white tower, as does the modest little archaeological museum, which you could easily miss if in a hurry. This museum, specialising in Macedonian treasures, is one of the newest of its kind in Greece and now has a spectacular collection of recent finds from Vergina, near Veria. They bear the star emblem of the Macedonian royal family and are believed to come from the tomb of Philip, Alexander's father. The exhibits include two big, gold caskets, silver ornaments and royal armour.

You can see all the sights of Thessalonika comfortably in a day, pausing on the way at some pleasant pavement cafes in green squares like Aristotleous, Thessalonika's answer to Athens' Syntagma. Others run off the city's main arteries, King Constantine Street, Alexander the Great Street, and Egnatius Street.

Thessalonika has good rail and air connections with Athens and western Europe, and its dominating position in the north-west corner of the Aegean makes it a natural gateway to Eastern Greece and the Halkidiki peninsula. The road east cuts across the top of Halkidiki, running by its lakes and fields of cotton, tobacco and wheat until it strikes Kavala, one of the most picturesque ports of mainland Greece. This is the place where Peter Ustinov sold souvenirs on the quayside at the start of 'Topkapi'. Houses rise from the harbour in an amphitheatre of colour crowned by a Byzantine castle and a grand Turkish aquaduct. Kavala seems to have all the waterside restaurants that Thessalonika mysteriously lacks and it is busy with ferries speeding off to Thassos and Lemnos. Phillipi, 15 kilometres north, is worth a visit to see the layout of a Graeco-Roman town with early churches. Between Kavala and Alexandropoulis there are some pleasant coves and sandy beaches, where rivers like the Nestos run into the sea, but Alexandropoulis is a place to speed through if you can. It is a departure point for ferries to Samothraki and Lemnos, but also a border town close to Turkey; full of soldiers, noisy, and short on scenic beauty.

Halkidiki, jutting out to the south-east of Thessalonika, is a place to linger in the right season. Its three spurs, Kassandra, Sithonia and Athos, stick out into the Aegean like Neptune's trident, vying with each other in green hills, pinewoods and long curving beaches. They are as good beaches as you find anywhere in Greece. Sand occasionally gives way to pebble, but the majority are long, golden and gently sloping into the sea. Amazingly, as you take the good coast roads, they emerge one after another round each promontory. No wonder the Greek National Tourist Organisation decided in the Sixties that they would start a special promotion of this area.

A well-deserved success story, as far as normal holiday pursuits go, but it has always seemed strange to me that an area that has such a powerful history, has little in the way of splendid archaeological sites. Most of the best finds are in the museum at Thessalonika. Little remains of old Macedonian towns like Olynthus and Potidea. Even Pella – the birthplace of Alexander – is not much more than a pile of stones in the corner of a ploughed field, and Vergina, with its temple and tomb, is

away south in central Greece. One other problem with Halkidiki is climate. For those who like beach holidays, its season runs little more than four summer months.

The road south from Thessalonika runs first to four local beach developments, and big camp sites, at Nea Epivates, Aghia Triada, Nea Mihaniona and Epanomi. All have reasonable beaches. You then have to branch inland to head for Kassandra and Sithonia, the western and middle legs of the Halkidikian crab, touching the coast again at Nea Kalikratia and Nea Moudania, which again boast more spectacular beaches.

Kassandra is reached via Potidea, with its ancient canal cutting the peninsula into the form of an island. Then the coast road soon divides into a loop that takes in all the pretty little fishing villages in the south of the peninsula.

Sithonia rivals Kassandra in wooded hills and sandy beaches. It also has a convenient loop road running right around the coast. Nikitas at the neck of Sithonia has long shingle beaches which turn into finer sand between Tripotamos and Neos Marmaras. The last is a lively village with numerous high standard restaurants and long beaches stretching away on both sides of the port.

One kilometre south of Neos Marmaras, John Carras, the shipping millionaire created an imaginative pleasure complex in the seventies called Porto Carras. This is the Port Grimaud of Greece. On a long beach backed by green hills stand three luxury hotels. Here, too, is a yacht marina, facilities for wind surfing and water skiing, nine first-class tennis courts (the best I have encountered in Greece) and a golf course. Porto Carras also boasts its own high quality wines, a casino and two theatres. Holidaymakers staying here, can hire small boats to explore the many nearby beaches, or take cruises to Toroni, Port Koufo and around Mount Athos.

Mount Athos

Europe's only monastic state, and the Greek answer to the Vatican, sits serene, remote and mysterious on the third prong of the trident that makes up Halkidiki. Mount Athos is a treasurehouse of religious history, with more relics of the New Testament story than are displayed in all the Catholic churches of Spain, Italy and Portugal.

The holy mountain, seldom visited in the past and never filmed, is almost unknown outside Greece. Yet it is a challenge to the fit and the adventurous that is now bringing more than a thin trickle of tourists east from Thessalonika.

From Ierissos and Ouranopolis, both among the biggest centres of population in Halkidiki, daily boats run along the two coasts of Mount Athos. With biblical symmetry, each coast has ten monasteries clinging to its hillsides and almost all of them can be seen from a passing boat. That's just as well for half the human race because there are strict limits on those setting foot on Mount Athos. You need, first, to be male, and, secondly, to have a visa from the appropriate ministry in Athens or Thessalonika. No woman has been on the mountain in ten centuries. If you have the right qualifications, you can then take the daily boat from Ouranopolis to the monastic state's only port at Daphne on the east coast, but bear in mind that cine cameras, like women, are forbidden on the holy mountain.

It is no chore to travel to Ouranopolis, which is presumably called 'City of the Sky' after the Byzantine watch tower that rises over the harbour. It is one of the pleasantest ports in Halkidiki with sandy beaches stretching away on both sides. A short caique ride away is the beautiful islet of Amouliani, boasting shining sandy coves and another small village. It is a shame that so many people treat Ouranopolis simply as a stepping stone to Athos, but the rise of tourism in the monastic state has at least brought new wealth to a village that previously relied heavily on poorly-paid rug-making. And six buses a day instead of two a week. The boat to Daphne takes two hours with stops at monastery harbours on the way. Then comes a bone-shaking bus trip to Karye, the village capital of Mount

Athos, where the Greek visa is exchanged for a residence permit, to be handed over to the receptionist monk at each monastery visited. It bears the seal and stamps of Athos.

The cost of entry was until recently 100 drachmas, but it has soared to 500 drachmas, with the only concession 300 drachmas for students. I have never seen so many 30 year olds protesting that they are students. By the time you have paid boat and bus fare, an overnight trip to Athos is expensive. But, if you stay two days or more, you get value for money. The monasteries provide simple board and lodging without charge, and will even supply a basic packed lunch – maybe just bread and olives – to anyone taking the long haul around Mount Athos itself. The paths between the monasteries are rough, varying from first class riverbed to stony track and there is no transport, apart from a few boatmen who ply the coastal routes in summer. So you need a strong pair of shoes.

The welcome from the monks is always friendly, but the board and lodging can be spartan and the atmosphere far from relaxing. Mount Athos is no holiday camp. Beds are in small dormitories and are hard. The sheets and blankets are not washed too often. Bathrooms are primitive and without toilet paper and mirrors. Curfew is at dusk, the monastery gates are locked, and the only light for reading is a shared oil lamp. Long before first light there is a dawn chorus of monks going to early services, summoned by bells and wooden drums at hourly intervals from around 3 am our time.

Mount Athos time is uncannily different. The day starts at dawn or dusk, depending on the monastery, and there is a charming vagueness about dates too. When I last visited Athos in mid-October, my residence permit was stamped '26 September'. Breakfast is a small, simple meal. Often coffee, water and a piece of Turkish delight. Evening meals, taken just before dusk, do not go much further than a plate of beans or soup, bread and olives, spiced with a glass of thick, fruity monastery wine. The culinary event of the day is lunch, which can run to three courses with cheese and fruit. But it too is simple.

For the dedicated, this is a small price to pay for the freedom to wander for four days in a land locked in time – or different times. The monasteries are like fortified museums teeming with frescoed chapels and row upon row of mediaeval icons. In one I visited the monks jokingly referred to their refectory as 'the bank' and carefully locked it behind visitors. Its walls were covered with golden icons dating back to the 10th Century, all numbered like those in the churches. There are no doubt rich men who wouldn't mind swapping their numbered bank accounts in Zurich for one of these.

What the march of history could not destroy is now gradually being eroded by an understanding lack of enthusiasm on the part of Greek youth to submit to the monastic discipline and isolation. From the 16th Century when there were 40,000 monks in 40 monasteries, there are now just over 1,000 monks in 20 monasteries, including one Bulgarian, one Serbian and one Russian community. A typical monastery resembles a small walled village with nine or ten separate churches and five-storey blocks of living quarters, but only twenty or thirty monks scattered about its spacious wings. Every church is festooned with icons and a few have greater treasures, such as pieces of the Holy Cross, solid gold bibles and pieces of clothing worn by the saints and Virgin Mary.

The Russian monastery, easily recognised by its green oriental bell towers and within easy walking distance of Daphne and Karye, claims to have the second biggest bell in the world. Cast in Moscow, it weighs in at 13,000 kilogrammes. Iviron, also close to the capital, boasts a solid silver lemon tree sent by the Tsar of Russia and a miraculous icon reputedly painted by one of the Apostles, which fell in the sea on arrival at Mount Athos. One of the monks was given a special dispensation, so the story goes, to walk on the water to retrieve the floating treasure.

The capital, Karye, is a pretty village with two small dusty restaurants and two hostels. It also houses the Government building, where the council of monks meet, and Protaton church, which is richly frescoed. The southern part, where the holy mountain slopes down to the sea, is a steep cliff where hermits and artists live. It is almost sheer and one look explains how the Persian invasion fleet was destroyed on the rocks in 483 BC. But there is a navigable track around the headland.

Travel

FLIGHTS	Up to 10 flights daily from Athens to Thessalonika (55 mins). Up to 2 flights daily from Athens to Kavala (1 hr 30 mins). Up to 2 flights daily from Athens to Alexandropoulis (55 mins).
TRAINS	Daily train service from Athens to Alexandropoulis via Thessalonika.
ROAD	Frequent buses from Athens to all parts of north-eastern Greece.
BOATS	This part of Greece has good and frequent ferry connections with all north-east Aegean islands, plus the Sporades and northern Dodecanese islands.

Information for Travellers

Some useful U.K. addresses
National Tourist Organisation of
Greece,
195 Regent Street,
London W1R 8DL.
Tel: 01-734 5997.

Greek Embassy,
1a Holland Park,
London, W.11
Tel: 01-727 8040

Hellenic Book Service,
122 Charing Cross Road,
London, W.C.2.
Tel: 01-836 7071.

The Mary Ward Centre &
The Mary Ward Greek Society,
42 Queens Square,
London, W.C.1.
Tel: 01-831 7711.
Promotes cultural understanding of
Greece through social meetings and
specialist language courses.

Thomson Holidays,
Greater London House,
Hampstead Road,
LONDON NW1 7SD.
Tel: 01-387 9321.
Leading Operator to Greece.

Passports
British visitors to Greece need an up-to-
date passport. This can be a regular British
Passport (valid 10 years) or a British
Visitors' Passport (valid one year only and
obtainable from post offices). No visa or
vaccination certificates are needed. The
same passport regulations apply to
nationals from: Eire, Australia, USA,
Canada, New Zealand and South Africa.
You can stay in Greece three months. If you
want to work you have to apply for the
special residence permit, valid for citizens
of the EEC.

Customs
Visitors entering Greece face normal
customs regulations on personal
belongings and duty-free goods. When
leaving Greece, the duty-free allowances
for UK residents are as follows:

Cigarettes	300
Cigars	75
Tobacco	400 grams
Spirits	1½ litres
Wine	4 litres
Perfume	75 grams
Money	1500 drachmas (approx £15)

As for souvenirs, you can take out virtually
what you like, **except** for any antiquities or
works of art (however small) found in
Greece. The penalties for illegal export of
antiquities are severe, and permits for
export have to be obtained from the
Archaeological Service, 13 Polygnotou
Street, Athens, or the Ministry of Culture
and Sciences.

Currency
Greece has an easy decimal currency
based on the drachma (dr). The five bank
notes come in denominations of 1,000, 500,
100 and 50 drachma. There are also six
main coins. The one and two dr coins are
bronze; the 50, 20, 10 and 5 dr coins are
nickel. Occasionally you will still find
50-lepta coins in circulation. These are
half-drachma and, as such, virtually
worthless.

Where to change money
Banks
Open Monday to Friday 0800 – 1400.
In main tourist centres some banks open
in the evenings and at weekends as well.

Banks will change foreign currency and travellers cheques. Eurocheques and personal cheques, backed by a Eurocard guarantee, can also be cashed in almost every branch of the Bank of Greece and other banks displaying the EC sign. Credit cards are not accepted. For any transaction your passport will be needed.

Hotels and Tavernas
Often even the smallest taverna in holiday centres will change foreign currency and travellers cheques. Usually only the large international hotels will take personal cheques and credit cards for payment.

Shops
Most shops catering for tourists will accept foreign currency or travellers cheques as payment. The rate of exchange won't be particularly good, though, and any change will be in drachmas.

Travel Agencies
Tickets can usually be paid for in foreign currency or travellers cheques. Credit cards and personal cheques are rarely accepted.

Where to get information and advice
The National Tourist Organization of Greece (NTOG) is the most obvious source of further information. Its worldwide offices will provide leaflets and maps on individual regions, plus lists of all hotels down to C grade. Make use of it, too, for up-to-date information on travel, festivals, museums and special festivities.

NTOG Information offices
London
National Tourist Organization of Greece
195-7 Regent Street
London W1R 8DR
Tel: 01-734 5997

Athens
1) (Head office)
2 Amerikas Street
Tel: 322311

2) 1 Voukourestiou Street
Tel: 3234467 (information on festivals)

3) 2 Karageorgi Servias Street,
Syntagma Square (inside National Bank)
Tel: 3222545

4) 4 Stadiou Street
Spyromiliou Arcade
Tel: 3221459

5) International Airport
Tel: 9799500

Piraeus
105 Vass Sofias Avenue
Tel: 4121400

Cephalonia
3 P. Vallianou Street
Metaxa Square
Tel: (0671) 22847

Corfu
The Governor's House
Tel: (0661) 39730

Crete
1) *Heraklion*
1 Xanthoudidou Street
Tel: (081) 282096 & 222487

2) *Chania*
6 Akti Tobazi
Tel: (0821) 26426

3) *Rethymnon*
100 Koundouritou Street
Tel: (0831) 29148

Evzoni
(road frontier office)
Tel: (0343) 51223

Igoumenitsa (summer only)
Limin Igoumenitsis
Tel: (0665) 22227

Ioannina
2 Nap Zerva Street
Tel: (0651) 25086

Kavala
2 Filellinon Street
Tel: (051) 228762 & 222425

Kipi Evrou
(road frontier office)
Tel: (0555) 31237

Kos
Akti Koundourioti
Tel: (0242) 28724

Larissa
18 Koumoundourou Street
Tel: (041) 250919

Niki
(road frontier office)
Tel: (0385) 92303

Patras
Iroon Politehniou Street, Glyfada
Tel: (061) 420304 & 420305

Promachon
(road frontier office)
Tel: (0323) 41241

Rhodes
Archbishop Makarios & Papagou Streets
Tel: (0241) 23655 & 23255

Thessalonika
1) 34 Metropoleos Street
Tel: (031) 271888 & 222935
2) Airport Information Office
Tel: 412261 ext. 021

Volos
Riga Ferraiou Square
Tel: (0421) 23500 & 24915

Tourist police
In Greece there's a helpful branch of the police called Tourist police. They have the same powers and duties as regular police, but their special authority is to help foreigners. Many have a knowledge of English and can give all kinds of assistance, ranging from accident emergencies to just finding accommodation. It is for the latter that Tourist police are especially useful. Their job is to know where accommodation exists, and in towns and on the islands they will have lists of people with rooms to let.

Remember, wherever you are in Greece the Tourist police telephone number is the same – 171.

British Embassy and Consulates
Athens
British Embassy
1 Ploutarchou Street
Tel: 736211

Corfu
Vice-Consulate
2 Zambeli Street
Tel: (0661) 30055 & 37995

Crete
Vice-Consulate
16 Papalexandrou Street
Heraklion
Tel: (081) 224102

Kavala
Vice-Consulate
45 Thessalonika Street
Tel: (051) 223704

Patras
Vice-Consulate
2 Votsi Street
Tel: (061) 277329

Rhodes
Vice-Consulate
23, 25th March Street
PO Box 47
Tel: (0241) 27247 & 27306

Samos
Vice-Consulate
Ag Theodorou Street
Port Vathy
Tel: (0273) 27314

Thessalonika
Consulate
11 Vass Konstantinou Avenue (3rd floor)
Tel: (031) 278169

Useful addresses in Athens
Lost Property
General
Tel: 4531716
Buses or Taxis
Tel: 5230111

Aliens Bureau
9 Halokokondilli Street
Tel: 3628301
Tel: 3622601 (for work and residence permits)

General Post Office
100 Eolou Street

British Airways
10 Othnos Street

OSE (Trains and Europabus)
1-3 Karolou Street
Tel: 5222491

ELPA – Automobile and Touring Club of Greece
Athens Towers
2-4 Messogion Street
Tel: 7791615

Motor Insurance Bureau
10 Zenofontos Street
Tel: 3236733

Medical advice

Full medical insurance is strongly advised for all visitors to Greece. In most cases you have to pay for the treatment at the time of illness/accident and then claim back the money from the insurance company after your return home. Employed people from the UK can get Form E111 from a Social Security Office before leaving Britain. In theory this entitles you to the same medical treatment as Greek citizens, but in practice much of this treatment is not nearly so comprehensive as you would find at home. Most main towns and islands have a hospital where you can obtain emergency treatment (Tel: 166 for information on local medical care). Otherwise, find a local doctor. In towns, cities and major tourist centres, this won't prove a problem, but in quieter rural areas it may be more difficult. In all cases the Tourist police (Tel: 171) should be able to advise you.

General insurance

It is usually cheaper to buy a comprehensive insurance which covers medical expenses, baggage loss or theft. If you do lose any of your personal belongings report it immediately to the police or Tourist police (Tel: 171).

Telephone

The Organismos Telephikinonion Eliathos (known as OTE) run the Greek telephone service. In small towns and villages there are public telephones at most post offices; in large towns the OTE offices are completely separate. Use kiosks, tavernas and shops for local calls. The owners are usually very obliging and will charge the standard rate of 4 dr. Whether at a public telephone, or those at hotels or tavernas, you pay for your call after you have made it, so you don't need a handful of small coins or tokens.

Useful Telephone Numbers

Directory enquiries	131
General information	134
International operator	161
Time	141
Medical care	166
City police	100
Country police	109
Coastguards	108
Tourist police	171
Fire	199
Roadside assistance (24 hours)	104

International Dialling Codes

In principle there is direct dialling from all telephones in Greece to almost anywhere in the world; in practice the system doesn't always work so well, and you need a lot of patience.

Australia	0061
Canada/USA	001
Great Britain/Eire	0044
New Zealand	0064

Telegrams

These can be sent from OTE offices or main post offices.

Post offices

Opening hours: 0800 - 1300 (APPROX) Buy your stamps at post offices or from kiosks and shops selling postcards. Current rate for postcard stamp to the UK is 21 dr. Post boxes are yellow and can be found in all towns and villages. Parcels and Post Restante letters can be collected from post offices, but remember to take your passport with you.

Shopping hours

Except in supermarkets and large shops there are definitely no set shopping hours in Greece. The rule to follow is that on the islands and country areas most provision shops open very early, close from approximately 1300 – 1600, and then open again for a few hours in the evening. On Sunday afternoons and Saints Days almost every shop is closed.

Tipping

Tipping is much the same as in the UK, but on a more modest scale. On the menus of most restaurants you will notice two prices for each item; the first is without service, the second with service. In most cases the second price is always charged so you only need to leave a few drachmas as tip after your meal.

Time change

Greek Standard Time is two hours ahead of GMT. Greek Summer Time corresponds almost exactly with British Summer Time (March – October) so the two-hour difference applies virtually all year round.

Local festivals

Music, drama and wine festivals are prominent features on the Greek summer and early autumn calender. These tend to be large, international affairs. For smaller, more intimate events, you will find that almost every island, town and village hold their own special festivals throughout the year. These are often held on the Saints Day of their church, or in some way relate to local history or activities such as fishing and wine making. Find out details of major festivals from the NTOG (addresses page 62) or get a copy of their useful publication, *General Information on Greece*.

Electricity

220 AC volt electricity is the standard supply, though a few remote areas are still on 110 DC volts. Two-pin plugs are widely used in Greece, so it is wise to buy an adaptor for hair dryers, electric shavers, etc.

Essential luggage

Even if you go on holiday in the middle of summer, evenings can be cool, especially in the Aegean when the Meltemmi blows. So, take something to cover up bare arms and legs. Open sandals are obviously practical for hot days, but if you want to walk anywhere except roads, pavements or beaches, then something stronger would be advisable. Antidotes to mosquitoes include insect repellant cream, calamine lotion and mosquito plugs and coils. The last are most effective and cheap and can be bought from Greek grocers shops. Medical equipment would wisely include antiseptic cream, a few plasters and the usual asprin and stomach upset remedies. If you do find the diet of rich oil a little too much, try a glass or two of undiluted lemon juice – it often seems to work. Towels are usually provided in hotels, but bring your own for the beach.

Opening times of museums

In summer most major museums and archaeological sites open at either 0800 or 0900 and stay open all day until 1900. Smaller museums usually have a 3-3½ hours closed period in the middle of the day. On Sundays and public holidays museums are open all year round from 1000 – 1630 and admission is free. Further details and exact opening times from the NTOG (addresses page 111).

Books and maps on Greece

Maps

The NTOG have a selection of free good-quality regional maps. Otherwise Edward Stanford Ltd, 12 Long Acre, London WC2 is recommended for more detailed Greek maps. In Athens try the National Statistical Service of Greece, 14 Likourgou.

Books

There are many books that have been written about Greece over the years. Everyone has their own tastes in travel literature, but in London, for a wide selection of books on Greece, we suggest you try the Hellenic Book Service, 122 Charing Cross Road, WC2, Tel: 01-836 7071, and Zeno Greek Bookshop, 6 Denmark Street, WC2. Tel: 01-836 2522. In Athens the best bookstore for English books on Greek subjects is Eseftheroudakis, 4 Nikis Street, Syntagma Square.

Internal travel

Ferries and Hydrofoils

In a country that's made up of over 1,000 islands, boats are obviously one of the main forms of internal transport. There are about 250 Greek ports in total, all with scheduled ferry connections. To find a comprehensive list of ferry timetables is not often easy, but the NTOG will usually be able to give some advice, or you could buy a copy of the monthly magazine 'Greek Travel Pages' available in the UK from Timsway Holidays, Penn Place, Rickmansworth, Herts, price £5 (inc p&p).

Once in Athens the NTOG office in Stadiou Street just off Syntagma Square issues a weekly information sheet on sailing times, routes and fares, or you can look at the shipping page of the English-language 'Athens News'. Piraeus is the main hub of shipping routes in the Aegean, and for detailed timetable information phone the Piraeus Port Authority, Tel: 4511311. The main islands have daily ferry connections all the year round; for the smaller, less tourist-oriented islands, ferry connections are not so numerous. And, remember, out of the main summer season, ferry services are reduced to the basic schedules, meaning that for some out-of-the-way islands there might be just one weekly connection. Prices and facilities on board vary according to size of boat and on which class you travel.

A long ferry journey can eat considerably into your holiday time and there are now several fast hydrofoil services, cutting sea travel times by anything up to 70 percent. These operate from Piraeus to the Saronic Islands and eastern Peloponnese; and in the Dodecanese from Rhodes to Kos, Patmos and Samos. There's a speed boat service in operation from Patras to Zakinthos and Cephalonia.

Air Travel

There is a good domestic air network in Greece. Operated by Olympic Airways, from Athens you can fly to 29 different destinations:
Aktion
Alexandroupolis
Cephalonia
Chios
Corfu
Crete: Heraklion, Chania
   and Rethymnon (via Chania)
Ioanina
Kalamata
Karvolassi (via Samos)
Kastoria
Kavala
Komotini (via Alexandroupolis)
Kos
Kozani
Kythera
Lemnos
Milos
Mykonos
Larissa
Lesbos
Paros
Rhodes
Samos
Santorini
Skiathos
Thessalonika
Zakinthos

Other routes:
Thessalonika – Lemnos
Thessalonika – Alexandroupolis
Thessalonika – Ionnina
Thessalonika – Kastoria
Thessalonika – Lesbos
Thessalonika – Skiathos
Rhodes – Karpathos
Rhodes – Kassos
Rhodes – Kos
Rhodes – Crete (Heraklion)
Rhodes – Mykonos
Santorini – Crete (Heraklion)
Santorini – Mykonos
Santorini – Rhodes
Mykonos – Crete (Heraklion)
Kastoria – Kozani

Some of these schedules are seasonal only and there are generally many more flights operating during the summer months. Despite considerable improvement over the past few years, over-booking still tends to be a problem during peak tourist months. So, the rule is to get to the airport early to ensure your seat. Information and air timetables from the NTOG, 'Greek Travel Pages', or Olympic Airways, 141 New Bond Street, W1. Tel: 01-493 7262.

CAR TRAVEL

When entering Greece with your own car, you have to show proof of third-party insurance. Comprehensive insurance is not essential, but is strongly recommended. The best plan is to obtain a Green Card (International Motor Insurance Certificate) from your insurance company at home before you leave. Also, as a useful precaution against bureacratic misunderstandings, it is wise to bring your vehicle registration papers as well. A British driving licence is sufficient – you do not need an international one.

Petrol

Greek petrol prices are about the same as those in the UK. It is wise to buy 'super' petrol; 'regular' Greek petrol can be of a very low octane rate. Service stations are plentiful around the main towns and tourist areas, but tend to be sparse in the more remote country areas. Take a spare petrol can for emergencies.

Roads

There are comparatively few motorways and high-speed routes in Greece. Roads in general vary from well-maintained tarmac to narrow dirt-tracks. On the latter, drive with care and look out for disguised potholes. Most main road signs are given in Greek and Latin characters, though sometimes – on country roads especially – neither seem to correspond with any of the spellings on your map.

Traffic rules

As in the rest of Europe, drive on the right and overtake on the left are the rules to remember. Otherwise road signs and signals are standard international and can easily be followed. Front seat belts are compulsory and there are now strong 'Drink and Drive' laws.

Breakdown

Carry essential spares and, if possible, your car's handbook. ELPA (The Automobile and Touring Club of Greece – address page 63) operate a good road breakdown service. Within 60 km of Athens, Thessalonika, Patras, Lamia and Larissa all you have to do is dial 104 for assistance (English is spoken by most officials). Contact ELPA for a full list of all their officials, in case you break down outside these main areas. Otherwise in cases of breakdown or accident, contact the main police or Tourist police (Tel: 171). The Motor Insurance Bureau, 10 Xenofondos Street, Athens (Tel: 3236733) can give useful information on all car insurance matters.

Buses

The Greek mainland is well served by buses, and long-distance bus travel is a cheap and simple way of getting around. The main bus terminal in Athens is at 100 Kifissou Avenue (just at the side of the Peloponnese railway station) and, from here, buses leave for all destinations in the Peloponnese and north and west Greece. Buses to Volos (for the Sporades) and Chalkis (for Evia) plus other destinations in central and eastern Greece leave from the 260 Liossion Street terminal (just at the side of the Larissa railway station). You buy a ticket before getting on board, or pay the driver if you are collected en route. Besides long-distance travel, buses are the mainstay of rural transport with daily services (often early morning) connecting outlying villages with nearby towns. In country districts there are usually no fixed bus stops; buses will stop by the roadside if you raise your hand. 'Greek Travel Pages' lists a comprehensive timetable of all main buses from Athens.

Trains

There are two railway lines in Greece. One serves the Peloponnese, with trains connecting Corinth, Patras and Kalamata. The other goes right up to Alexandroupolis in the north-eastern corner of the country via Larissa and Thessalonika. There are frequent services to all these places but, in general, though train travel is cheap in Greece, it is slow and not very comfortable.

From Athens: trains to the Peloponnese leave from Stathmos Peloponnisos; trains to the north leave from Stathmos Larissis.

Taxis

On the islands and in mainland country area, taxis are an important form of transport and are used for even quite long journeys. Though not as cheap as they were, fares are still low by our standards. In towns fares will be shown on a meter. In country areas you pay by the kilometre, though for longer journeys it is wiser to try and arrange the fare in advance to save any misunderstanding later.

Coach Tours
Wherever you are in Greece, coach tours can often prove to be the quietest and best way of sightseeing. Many companies operate these tours. In Athens the main ones are:
CHAT Tours, 4 Stadiou Street
ABC, 47 Stadiou Street
Key Tours, 2 Ermou Street
American Express,
15-17 Venizelou Street

Car Rental
Many British package tours organise special car rental deals for their clients. If you can arrange this, it is usually the cheapest way of hiring a car when on holiday. Otherwise, there are plenty of car rental firms throughout Greece, including the main holiday islands. The NTOG in London can provide a list of companies but, once in Greece, you will easily be able to find the names of local firms. Rates vary, but renting a car in Greece is not often a cheap exercise. The main problem is that, even though they look fairly reasonable, rates quoted hardly ever include the 18 per cent charged for local taxes and collision damage insurance.

Scooters and Motorbikes
Scooters are an ideal way of summer holiday travel. Especially on the islands where the distances aren't great. Most islands and mainland centres organise scooter hire and the rates are not expensive. On a scooter or motorbike, you can explore small paths and tracks vetoed to cars and often discover the unspoilt and unknown beaches. But, take out a good insurance policy and drive carefully on the unmadeup roads.

Bicycles
Cycling has never really caught on in Greece. The terrain is too mountainous and the summer climate too hot to deter all but the real enthusiast. However, you can usually rent a bicycle cheaply on most of the developed islands and, if you have your own, ferries hardly ever charge for transporting it.

Yachts
Yachts of any nationality entering Greek waters must first put in at one of the 27 official ports of entry. The NTOG information sheet on 'Provisions for Foreign Flag Yachts' calling at Greek Ports' gives information on yachting formalities. Upon arrival in port, the skipper should apply for a transit log which will entitle the yacht to unlimited travel in Greek waters and the crew members to buy duty-free fuel, alcohol and cigarettes. The Greek radio network transmits weather bulletins in English every day at 0635.

Early and late summer holidays are especially recommended if you want to sail round the Aegean islands. In mid-summer, from July to September, the Meltemmi blows almost consistently. This is a strong, blustery north wind that doesn't make for plain sailing.

SPORTS FOR ALL

In a country that is surrounded by so much sea, water sports take a natural precedence over all others in Greece. At most of the 19 NTOG public beaches (get a list from any NTOG office) facilities include swimming pools, canoes, pedaloes, wind surfing, tennis courts, water skiing and playgrounds for children. At other main holiday centres you will also find plenty of sports and facilities to choose from.

Wind Surfing
Now one of the most popular sports in all Greece. At every main centre you will be able to hire boards and get some kind of instruction. For details, of Greek wind surfing centres contact the London Wind Surfing Centre, 553 Battersea Park Road, London SW11. Tel: 01-223 2590, or the Hellenic Wind Surfing Association, 7 Filelinon Street, Athens (Tel: 3230068).

Water Skiing

Water skiing has been taken over in popularity by wind surfing, but it is still much in evidence, especially round Attica and islands such as Crete, Rhodes, Corfu, Skiathos and Poros. Prices tend to be on the expensive side. For general information apply to the Water Ski Federation, 32 Stournara Street, Athens (Tel: 5231875).

Sailing

Some villages and many beaches can only be reached by boat. Find someone to take you where you want to go (for a fee) or, alternatively, rent a dinghy for yourself. Many centres have all types of sailing boats for hire. For Greek island and flotilla cruising, there are many tour operators and companies specialising in this type of holiday. Some holidays come with a cook and crew; others just provide a boat and skipper, leaving the crewing for you and others.

Snorkelling

The clear Greek seas are made for underwater swimming. Bring your own snorkelling equipment or buy it inexpensively in most seaside villages. Snorkelling is permitted almost everywhere, including fishing with a speargun, though it is illegal to catch fish weighing less than 150 gm (5 oz).

Archaeological remains found underwater should not be disturbed and any discoveries reported to the authorities.

Scuba Diving

Underwater swimming and fishing with compressed air equipment is only permitted in a few areas of Greece and in these permission can only be given by the naval authorities or captain of the port. Find out details from the NTOG circular dealing with underwater fishing. Underwater diving schools operate from the Hellenic Federation of Underwater Activities in Athens, Thessalonika, Corfu, Piraeus and Rhodes.

Fishing

Sea fishing is a popular sport – especially in summer and autumn – and boats and tackle can be rented almost anywhere.

Permits are not required. Information from: Amateur Anglers and Maritime Sports Club, Moutsopoulou Quay, Piraeus (Tel: 4515731). Carp, eel and crayfish can be found in the lakes, and trout in some rivers. However, freshwater fishing is very limited in Greece. Again, no permits are needed.

Golf

Greece has only five main golf courses. These are at:

Glifada (Athens)
Rhodes
Corfu
Halkidiki
Skiathos

Horse Riding

Besides expensive equestrian clubs in Attica, Thessalonika and Corfu, riding in Greece is mostly confined to donkeys and mules. These are available for hire in many villages throughout the country but, surprisingly, prices are not often cheap.

Tennis

Public tennis courts are rare, though many large international hotels, campsites and NTOG beaches have courts. Equipment is not usually provided.

Hunting

The shooting season for quail, partridge, woodcock, waterfowl, hare and wild boar is from August to March. There are no private estates or game reserves in Greece and hunting is permitted on all open ground for a fee. To import a shotgun, make sure the number is on your passport. Information from: Ministry of Agriculture, 3-5 Ipocratsus Street, Athens.

Walking and Climbing

Some rambling holidays are organised from Britain, especially during the spring and autumn months. For hill walking and climbing the rugged mountains of central Greece and Crete could prove a considerable challenge. There are a welcome number of refuge huts dotted around the high mountainous areas and information on these, plus details of routes and hire equipment can be obtained from the:

Greek Touring Club
12 Polytechniou Street
Athens
Tel: Athens 5248601

The Federation of Excursion Clubs of Greece
4 Dragatsaniou Street
Athens
Tel: Athens 3234107

The Greek Skiing and Alpine Association
7 Karagiorgi Servias Street
Athens
Tel: Athens 3234555

Skiing
Skiing in Greece is now a popular winter sport. There are small ski centres all over the high central mountains (plus one in Crete) open yearly from December to March. Information from: The Greek Skiing and Alpine Association (address above).

Cave Exploring
Thousands of caves and underground waterways have been discovered in Greece. Only a very small percentage are open to the public, but those that are present amazing displays of underground phenomena. NTOG offices can give information and details.

Spectator Sports
For a country that spawned the Olympic Games, organised sports are not much in evidence. Football is now the main attraction with every town and village boasting its own local team. The one course for horse-racing is in Athens and it is the capital, too, that attracts motor racing enthusiasts for the annual Acropolis Rally.

Useful phrases
In Athens, main towns and all but the smallest islands, English (of sorts) is spoken. So, you can really get by on a holiday in Greece without knowing much Greek. However, it is always useful to understand, or recognise, some important words and phrases in any language, and we have selected what we consider are the essentials. For anything more specific, buy a good phrase book and/or a dictionary.

SOME USEFUL PHRASES . . .

English	Transliteration	Greek
How are you?	Ti kanete	Τί κάνετε;
Fine, thank you, and you	Kala, efkaristo, kee sees	Καλά, εὐχαριστῶ, καί σεῖς
What is that?	Ti, eeneh afto	Τί εἶναι αὐτό;
Do you speak English?	Milate Anglika	Μιλᾶτε Ἀγγλικά;
How much is it?	Poso kani afto	Πόσο κάνει; ὑτό
That's too expensive	eeneh poli ahkreeva	Εἶναι πολύ ἀκριβά
I don't understand Greek	Then katalaveno hellinika	Δέν καταλαβαίνω Ἑλληνικά
I want to go to . . .	Thelo na pao sto . . .	Θέλω νά πάω στό ...
Where is . . .	Pou ine	Ποῦ εἶναι
What time is it?	Ti ora ine	Τί ὥρα εἶναι
Can I have . . .?	Boro nah ekko	Μπορῶ νά ἔχω...;
Please give me . . .	Parakalo, dhoste mou	Παρακαλῶ, δῶστε μου
Could you speak more slowly, please?	Boreetah na milate pio siga, parakalo	Μπορεῖτε νά μιλᾶτε πιό σιγά, παρακαλῶ
a single room	ena mono dhomateeo	ἕνα μονό δωμάτιο
a double room	ena diplo dhomateeo	ἕνα διπλό δωμάτιο
with twin beds	meh dio krevatia	μέ δύο κρεββάτια
with balcony, shower	meh balkoni, doos	μέ μπαλκόνι, ντούς
Where are the toilets?	Pou ine i toualettes	Ποῦ εἶναι οἱ τουαλέττες
I'll be staying three days	Tha meeno tris imeres	Θά μείνω τρεῖς ἡμέρες
I am, we are	eemi, eemaste	εἶμαι, εἴμαστε
I have, we have	echo, echoume	ἔχω, ἔχουμε

English	Transliteration	Greek
I don't know yet	Then ksero akoma	Δέν ξέρω ἀκόμα
No, I don't like it	Okhi, then mou aresee	Ὄχι, δέν μοῦ ἀρέσει
Have you any stamps	Echete grahmatosemah	Ἔχετε γραμματόσημα
Walking	meh ta podeea	μέ τά πόδια
Can we camp here?	Boromeh na kataskenosomeh edo	Μποροῦμε νά κατασκηνώσουμε ἐδῶ;
Where is the tourist information centre?	Pou eeneh to touristiko grafeeo	Ποῦ εἶναι τό τουριστικό γραφεῖο;
The bill, please	Ton logaryasmo, parakalo	Τόν λογαριασμό, παρακαλῶ
This is not fresh	Afto then ine fresko	Αὐτό δέν εἶναι φρέσκο

SOME USEFUL WORDS . . .

English	Transliteration	Greek
Yes, no	neh, okhi	ναί, ὄχι
Yes (more formal or with emphasis)	malista	μάλιστα
Please, thank you	parakalo, efkaristo	παρακαλῶ, εὐχαριστῶ
Thank you very much	efkaristo polie	εὐχαριστῶ πολύ
Welcome, excuse me, pardon, what, watch out (no exact English meaning)	oriste	ὁρίστε
Good morning, day	kaleemera	καλημέρα
Good evening	kalee spera	καλησπέρα
Good night	kaleenikta	καληνύχτα
Excuse me, I'm sorry	signomi	συγνώμη
Hello	yasou	γειά σου
Goodbye	adio	ἀντίο
The (singular and plural)	o, ee, to	ὁ, ἡ, τό
	ee, ee, ta	οἱ, οἱ, τά
Where, when	pou, pote	ποῦ, πότε
How, who	pos, pios	πῶς, ποιός
Why, because	yiati, dioti	γιατί, διότι
What, nothing	ti, tipota	τί, τίποτα
Good, bad	kalos, kakos	καλός, κακός
Big, small	megalo, mikro	μεγάλος, μικρός
left, right	aristera, dexia	ἀριστερά, δεξιά
cheap, dear	fthino, akrivo	φθηνός, ἀκριβός
hot, cold	zesto, krio	ζεστός, κρύος
open, closed	anikto, klisto	ἀνοικτός, κλειστός
fast, slow	grigora, sigar	γρήγορα, σιγά
very good	poli kalo	πολύ καλός
new, old	neo, palio	νέος, παλιός
far, near	makria, konta	μακρυά, κοντά
Entrance, exit	issodos, exodos,	εἴσοδος, ἔξοδος
Museum, post office	mousseo, takidromio	μουσεῖο, ταχυδρομεῖο
Hotel, restaurant	xenodokio, estiatorio	ξενοδοχεῖο, ἑστιατόριο
Bank, church	trapeza, ekleesia	τράπεζα, ἐκκλησία
Ruins, toilet	archea, tooaleta	ἀρχαία, τουαλέττα
Bus, stop	leoforio, stasis	λεωφορεῖο, στάσις
Train, station	traino, stathmos	τραῖνο, σταθμός
Danger, take care	kindino, prosekete	κίνδυνος, προσέκετε
Upper, lower	ano, kato	ἄνω, κάτω
Beach, sea	paralia, thalassa	παραλία, θάλασσα

Aeroplane, airport	aeroplano, aeroporto	ἀεροπλάνο, ἀεροδρόμιο
Ship, small boat	vapori, varka	βαπόρι, βάρκα
At, in (side)	sto, mesa	στό, μέσα
To, from	pros, ahpo	πρός, ἀπό
After, before	meta, prin	μετά, πρίν
And, or	ki, ee	καί, ἤ
Here, there	edo, eki	ἐδῶ, ἐκεῖ
Now, then	tora, tote	τώρα, τότε
With, without	meh, horis	μέ, χωρίς
One, two	ena, dio	ἕνα, δύο
Three, four	tria, tessera	τρία, τέσσερα
Five, six	pende, exi	πέντε, ἕξι
Seven, eight	efta, okto	ἐφτά, ὀκτώ
Nine, ten	ennea, deka	ἐννέα, δέκα
Twenty, fifty	ikosi, peninda	εἴκοσι, πενήντα
Hundred, thousand	ekato, hilia	ἑκατό, χίλια
Sunday, Monday	kiriaki, deftera	Κυριακή, Δευτέρα
Tuesday, Wednesday	triti, tetarti	Τρίτη, Τετάρτη
Thursday, Friday	pempti, paraskevi	Πέμπτη, Παρασκευή
Saturday, today	Savato, simera	Σάββατο, σήμερα
Month, week	mina, evdomada	μήνα, ἑβδομάδα
Morning, evening	proi, vradi	πρωῖ, βράδυ
food and drink	fayita kee pota	φαγητό καί ποτά
table, menu	trapezi, katalogos	τραπέζι, κατάλογος
glass, bottle	potiri, bukali	ποτήρι, μπουκάλι
beer, wine	bira, krassi	μπύρα, κρασί
salt, pepper	alahti, piperi	ἁλάτι, πιπέρι
oil, lemon	lahdi, lemoni	λάδι, λεμόνι
bread, butter	psomi, vutiro	ψωμί, βούτυρο
coffee, tea	kafes, tsai	καφές, τσάϊ
jam, honey	marmelada, meli	μαρμελάδα, μέλι
eggs, fried	avga, tiganita	αὐγά, τηγανητά
milk, sugar	gala, zahkaree	γάλα, ζάχαρη
water, lemonade	nero, lemonada	νερό, λεμονάδα
ice cream, yoghurt	pahgoto, yaouriti	παγωτό, γιαούρτι
soup, fish	soupa, psari	σούπα, ψάρι
mullet, lobster	barbouni, astakos	μπαρμπούνι, ἀστακός
meat, cheese	kreas, tiri	κρέας, τυρί
beef, veal	vodino, moskari	βοδινό, μοσχάρι
pork, chicken	hirino, kotopoulo	χοιρινό, κοτόπουλο
lamb, suckling pig	arnaki, gurunopoulo	ἀρνάκι, γουρουνόπουλο
ham, sausage	zambon, loukaniko	ζαμπόν, λουκάνικο
salad, tomatoes	salata, tomates	σαλάτα, ντομάτες
potatoes, beans	patates, fasolia	πατάτες, φασολ
omelet	omehletah	ὀμελέττα
fruit, apples	fruita, milia	φρούτα, μῆλα
grapes, melon	stafilia, peponi	σταφύλια, πεπόνι
resinated wine, ouzo	retsina, uzo	ρετσίνα, οὖζο

Main Dates in Greek History

Greek history is a story of countless invasions and occupations, reflecting the country's position on the ancient anvil of civilisation and the modern crossroads of Europe and Asia. These ebbs and flows of wars and conquests gave birth to European civilisation.

Greek history is well documented because writers like Homer and Herodotus recorded events at length. Their contemporaries in Egypt and Mesopotamia were using their papyruses mostly for palace inventories and limiting their versions of great events to brief inscriptions on stone.

The first 1200 years from around 1500 BC to 300 BC were largely concerned with the unification of Greece, with the city states sometimes fighting among themselves, sometimes uniting to fight the eternal war with Asia. Most of the time from then to the Second World War, Greece has been occupied by a series of foreign invaders; the Romans, the Crusaders, the Venetians, the Turks, the Italians and the Germans. It is only since 1949 that the country has been really free and united, and even during the last 30 years there has been the shadow of military dictatorship, the troubles in Cyprus and the arguments with Turkey over Aegean oil rights.

It is no wonder that the Greek people are so fatalistic, and only surprising that they still offer such warmth and hospitality towards strangers.

BC

3000-1500 The Minoans rule the Eastern Mediterranean from Crete.

1150 Mycenae, dominant in Greece, leads the siege and sack of Troy supported by Sparta, Pylos and the Ionian Islands.

850 Homer of Chios composes 'The Iliad' and 'Odyssey'. City states such as Athens, Corinth, Samos, Mytileni and Samos emerge.

776 First Olympic games between city states.

734 Greek colonisation of Corfu, Sicily, Asia and Black Sea.

664 First sea battle between Corinth and her colony Corfu.

650 Age of tyrants and law-makers, including Dracon in Athens.

546 Persian conquest of Asiatic Greeks.

512 First Persian invasion of Europe. Darius conquers Thrace.

499-497 Ionian revolt and burning of Sardis.

490 Darius invades Greece, and is beaten by Athenians and allies at Marathon.

483 Persians under Xerxes hew canal through Chalcidice.

480 Xerxes invades Greece. Spartans die delaying Persians at pass of Thermopylae, but Persian fleet is destroyed by Athenians at Salamis.

479 Greek army led by Sparta wins battle of Plataea.

478 Athens founds confederation of Delos to unify Greeks. The Golden Age or Age of Pericles begins, with writings of Herodotus, Sophocles,

Aeschylus; concept of 'democracy' and colonisation of Aegean.

459 Athenian expedition to Egypt. Building of long walls to Piraeus.

454 Egyptian expedition fails. Transfer of treasury of Delos to Athens.

448 Peace with Persia. Athens loses Thebes at battle of Coronea.

431 The Peloponnesian War breaks out between Athens and Sparta. First Peloponnesian invasion of Attica.

429 Death of Pericles.

422 Battle of Emphipolis leads to peace of Nicias and defensive alliance between Athens and Sparta.

418 Sparta wins battle of Mantinea. Athens isolated.

415 Athenian expedition to Sicily, Siege of Syracuse.

405 Battle of Aegospotami decides fate of Peloponnesian War.

404 Athens surrenders and long walls demolished, but culture flourishes under Socrates, Euripides, Plato, Aristotle, Aristophanes, Thucydides and Xenophon.

401 Cyrus revolts against Artaxerxes with 10,000 Greek troops, but is killed at Cunaxa. The 10,000 march back.

395 Alliance of Thebes and Athens against Sparta.

374 Peace between Athens and Sparta.

371 Emerging power of Thebes nearly defeats Sparta at Leuctra.

369 Thebans invade Peloponnese.

364 Thebes defeats Athenian allies at Cynoscephalae.

362 Peace after Thebes defeats Spartan and Athenian armies.

358 Philip of Macedon starts conquest of northern cities. Aegean isles revolt against Athens.

356 Birth of Alexander.

351 Demosthenes rallies Athenians against Philip.

342 Philip conquers Thrace.

338 Philip defeats combined Greek armies at Chaeronea.

336 Macedonians invade Asia, but Philip is murdered. Accession of Alexander, who is elected general of the Greeks.

334 Alexander invades Persia. Battle of Granicus. Conquers Asia Minor.

333 Alexander at Gordion, cuts the sacred knot.

332 Alexander conquers as far as the Hindu-Kush.

323 Death of Alexander. Greece revolts against Macedonia.

300 Hellenistic Age starts. Colossus of Rhodes erected.

200 Roman legions on the borders of Greece

146 Corinth invaded. Greece becomes a Roman province with Athens the leading university of the Empire.

AD

340 The Roman Empire divides into East and West. Greece becomes a province of Byzantium or Constantinople.

527 Justinian becomes Emperor and law-giver, wins back Italy, Spain and North Africa. The great age of Byzantium follows.

1204 The Crusaders invade Greece. Many islands fall to Venice and parts of the mainland to the Franks and Normans. Sack of Constantinople.

1261 Greeks retake Constantinople.

1309-1523 The Knights of St John occupy Rhodes and Kos.

1453 Emerging power of Turkey takes Constantinople. Scholars flee to Italy. Greece in eclipse for four centuries.

1466 and 1687 Venice briefly win back Athens from Turks while ruling Crete.

1716 Venice retains Corfu after Turkish assault, but again loses Athens other Ionian isles and Peloponnese to Turks.

1770 Russia captures some Aegean isles from Turks.

1797 France wins Venice and with it Corfu.

1813 Treaty of Paris gives Corfu and Ionian isles to Britain.

1821 Greece revolts against Turkey in War of Independence which lasts 12 years.

1822 Turks crush revolt on some islands, massacre of Chios.

1824 Death of Lord Byron during Greek War of Independence.

1833 Last Turks evicted from Athens, which becomes capital of Greece.

1863 Ionian isles ceded peacefully to Greece.

1912 Italy defeats Turks and wins Dodecanese under Treaty of Lausanne.

1913 Crete and north-east Aegean isles join Greece after Balkan Wars.

1914-1918 Greece on Allied side in First World War, wins back more territory.

1919 The Greeks take Izmir (Smyrna) and war with Turkey follows.

1922 Kemal Ataturk retakes Izmir.

1936-1940 Greece under military rule of Metaxas, who says "no" to Mussolini.

1939-1945 Greece again on the Allied side in World War Two. Occupied by Italians and Germans for much of war.

1945-1948 Dodecanese liberated by British forces and reunited with Greece.

1947-1949 Savage civil war ending in Communist defeat.

1967 Military dictatorship of Colonels under Papadopoulos suppresses democracy. King Constantine leaves Greece after abortive attempt to restore democracy.

1973 Restoration of democracy under Karamanlis, but Greeks vote against return of king and Turkey invades northern Cyprus, redividing island with Attila line, so that Turkish part includes Kyrenia and Famagusta.

1981 Greece joins Common Market. First Socialist Government under Papandreou's Pasok party.

Modern Greece

Greece joined the Common Market in 1981 in a bid to join the modern world and revive a tired economy, whose rapid growth in recent years has been hit by hyperinflation, stagnation and rising unemployment. In the same year, looking for a New Deal on NATO and the EEC, it elected a socialist government under the leadership of Andreas Papandreou.

Since then Greece has been a rebel voice in the EEC, but has stuck to rocking the boat rather than sinking it. The advantages of staying in the Common Market are too many to justify quitting.

It might sound boringly like Britain ten years on – and there are some similarities – but the differences are more apparent. Many say modern Greeks bear no relationship to their ancient forebears who plundered Troy, invented mathematics and wrote great tragedies. They have a foot in the Middle East and also in the Middle Ages.

The reason why Greece's stake in the EEC may be working the miracles that have evaded Britain is that it is largely a low-wage, agricultural economy. Some Greek farmers are finding their poor peasant existence transformed by guaranteed prices, regional development grants, new roads and rich new markets in western Europe, as the farmers of France and Ireland did before them.

For the holidaymaker, there's good news and bad news. The good news is that you can now walk unscathed through the green Customs channel on the way home, with the full EEC allowance of drink, tobacco and perfume. That means just about as much as you can carry provided you buy in local shops and not the duty-free at the airport. It's a crazy allowance; with the full quota of seven bottles per person (or seven litres, if all wine) you could break your wrists and end up paying excess baggage.

The bad news is that prices in Greece have taken a sharp jump upwards during the first four years the country has been in the Common Market. The cost of rooms, restaurant meals, boat fares and motor bike hire have soared as much as 50 per cent on some islands, and prices are still rising between 20 and 30 per cent a year. Fortunately for British and US holidaymakers, the strength of the pound and dollar and the weakness of the drachma have provided a cushion against the worst impact of spiralling prices in Greece, and the country is still amazingly cheap compared with ours.

Also standards are rising with prices. Greek bathrooms have long been the butt of bad jokes, famed for their permawet floors, corrugated toilet paper, non-flush loos, reversible taps, porous plugs and a choice of cool and cold running water. Now, many of the humblest island dwellings have showers and, thanks to the spread of solar heating in Greece, also have hot water for at least some hours of the day.

Even in the 1980's it is questionable whether EEC regulations make sense to, or are, readily adopted by, villages whose main form of transport is the donkey, and where grain is still crushed by a large circular millstone in the manner of 2,000 years ago. Will Greece be able to preserve the fragile democracy that has existed since the six-year rule of the Colonels? Modern history has shown democracy sitting oddly on the country which invented it. It has been interspersed at regular intervals by military dictatorship and guarded by a royal rule under German monarchs, which the Greeks did not hesitate to ditch in a referendum when they had the chance.

The answer to all these questions is that Greece will almost certainly adapt, as it has in the past, to the trappings of the modern world without quickly sacrificing its links with the past. The donkey loaded with olives already trots obediently to the side of the road to allow the passage of a modern tour bus or a lorry ladened with sanitaryware. The small fisherman already gives way to island hydrofoils and looks up curiously at passing jet airliners without being persuaded he should wear shoes or mechanise beyond a simple chug-chug engine.

Cafe life clicks on with its ritual of tiny cups, cards, and ancient backgammon sets, despite the huge ornamental TV set that now transforms evenings into mass viewing of football matches and despite hordes of tourists who descend in scanty costumes. Bus drivers turn the fronts of their vehicles into small religious shrines festooned with miniature icons and taxi-drivers often play with worry-beads, like old men in the cafe. There are more little white churches than ever in Greece, and rising prosperity will inspire the building of yet more. The priests still wear their black tophats and have their hair drawn back in a knot, even though they now travel in a Mercedes and wear imported shoes.

The old skin or bladder water bottle, which works magnificently in cooling down its contents because it leaks a little which evaporates and cools the surrounding air, still hangs on a door post, while across the way a shop is richly hung with plastic containers. No society in the modern world has taken to plastic in quite the way that the Greeks have.

Greece needs its tourists, its ships and its migrant workers overseas. The Greek fleet is the biggest in the world. A country of 9½ million people controls one-eighth of the world's merchant fleet, and roughly twice as many ships as Britain. The reasons are partly tradition, based on 200 shipping families from most of the islands of the Aegean and the nouveau riche like the tanker-owning Onassis and Niarchos families. They are also partly based on cheap crews and cheap ships. It is not unusual to find a British, German or Swedish name painted over on a Greek island ship. Alas, the huge Greek fleet is not based on good seamanship. Its safety record is poor, and not only because it uses so many second-hand ships. Greek losses at sea are about three times the world average. Fortunately for tourists though, the passenger shipping authorities have tightened up a lot in the last fifteen years.

Little has changed in the life of Greek island fishermen in the past century. Their ships have engines, so they can go further from port, but most toil laboriously for hours on tangled nets and then bring in but two bucketloads of small fish after a night at sea. Many times I have heard the argument that the Mediterranean is over-fished and the Greeks only get the scraps left over by the Spaniards and Italians. The same argument is sometimes used to justify the massive mark-ups of fish in smart and not-so-smart restaurants, which often make fish twice as dear on the table as meat that has taken years of painstaking husbandry and feeding on a farm. There is a grain of truth in all this, but it has become enlarged into a modern Greek myth; part of the strange fish culture or folklore that Greece fosters. If you plunge into the sea off any Greek harbour or island with snorkel equipment, you will find yourself in a delightful natural aquarium surrounded by fish, much of it edible.

A sad, casualty of modern Greece is pollution. The sea has been used as the ultimate sewer and waste disposal unit of civilisation since time immemorial, but it cannot handle modern refuse like oil, plastic and chemicals. Some of the best sand beaches are already badly scarred by great globules of tar as a result of facing shipping lanes on which waste is being carelessly dumped from ships. And you have to go a long way along the so-called Athenian Rivieira coast to avoid cloudy seas that seem to match the haze of pollution that often hangs in the air over the whole Athens-Piraeus area.

But, pollution does not stop there. Some of the popular islands are suffering from a plague of plastic, both on the beaches and in the sea. It is dumped by ships, residents and tourists alike. So far the island authorities have done little to combat this problem. On the contrary. Many use a convenient steep seaside cliff as their local rubbish dump. Sometimes a crude attempt is made to burn rubbish, before it rolls down into the sea. I wonder how bad this problem has to become before more enlightened methods are employed. It is clearly in the interest of a country gaining such a massive inflow of money from tourism to spend more on rubbish collection and cleaning and to bring in tougher laws on pollution on land and at sea. Fortunately, this problem is still marginal, and may even go unnoticed by the majority of visitors to Greece. But it is curious that it can co-exist with a society that almost makes a fetish of household cleanliness, turns out its children in spotless clothes and devotes much time to tending churches and wayside shrines.

Happily, it detracts little, as does tourism, from the gentle, measured pace of island life which has gone on in the same way for generations past. The fisherman casting his nets in a quiet bay, the farmer trotting along on his donkey, the old men chatting for hours over coffee in the cafe. On a recent visit to a favourite island pension I witnessed a meeting to debate the advisability of a new road. A Minister flew to the island from Athens and came across the bay by boat to sound out local opinion.

In Britain it would have been a mundane affair in a church hall, but in Greece it was turned into a festival. The fatted goat was killed for the occasion. Long tables were covered with flowers and bottles of beer, soft drinks and retsina and everyone dressed in their best clothes. Half an hour before the Minister arrived the hills and coast suddenly became alive with people walking and on donkeys travelling to the great event. Some came by boat. When the Minister arrived there was a heated debate for no more than fifteen minutes, then the decision was clear. There would be a road. Everyone fell to eating and drinking, with former opponents chatting happily away, shaking hands and toasting the decision.

Contemporary Greek culture is a strange mixture of ancient and modern. The country and the people seem to be able to adapt, with their age-old fatalism and hospitality, to anything new without it disturbing their essential life-style. That is the glory that is modern Greece.

Personal Recommendations

Families Corfu, Zakynthos, Kos
Golfers Rhodes, Corfu, Skiathos
Motor Cyclists Corfu, Rhodes, Lesbos
Cyclists Aegina, Kos, Corfu
Campers Evia, Thassos, Crete
Motorists Crete, Evia, Peloponnese
Walkers Kythera, Kithnos, Serifos
Windsurfers Corfu, Rhodes, Evia
Naturalists Santorini, Nissiros, Lesbos
Students Crete, Thassos, Naxos
Back-packers Ios, Naxos, Crete
Hermits Patmos, Amorgos, Mount Athos
Painters Hydra, Mykonos, Santorini
Wine Buffs Samos, Santorini, Cephalonia
Beach Bums Skiathos, Antiparos, Naxos
Culture Vultures Delos, Peloponnese, Santorini
Nudists Mykonos, Crete, Rhodes
Gays Mykonos, Hydra, Skiathos
Teeny-boppers Ios, Spetse, Corfu
Trend-setters Skiathos, Hydra, Paros
Plutocrats Rhodes, Skiathos, Mykonos
Honeymooners Rhodes, Skiathos, Corfu
Island Hoppers Western Cyclades, Eastern Cyclades, Dodecannese
Seasoned Travellers: Cephalonia, Karpathos, Lesbos
Solitaries Amouliani, Inoussa, Aghios Efstratios
Masochists Antikythera, Salamis, Poros
The rest of us Milos Folegandros, Patmos

Sunset in Paros

Thomson-the complete story of Greece...from Athens to Zakynthos

From the beginning of civilisation, the ancient Greeks have speculated on the meaning of life and the nature of reality . . . But the Thomson Greek philosophy holds no such mystery. We are presenting, quite simply, the greatest range of Greek holidays ever! And with eight brochures to choose from, there's no reason to leave your holiday plans in the lap of the gods.

In our 'A La Carte' brochure, you'll see some of the finest hotels in Greece, while young people will find themselves amongst like minds in the 'Freestyle' range.

The choice of hotels in 'Summer Sun' meanwhile, is as classic as ever.

If you're looking for the freedom of your own holiday home, you'll find a choice of locations from Corfu to Skiathos: 'Villas and Apartments'

But in all brochures, the best discoveries you'll make are our prices. So turn over a new leaf with Thomson in Greece this summer.

A range of hotels to suit every taste

The Big T Club for children

Young Fun holidays for a lively time

Action Packed hotels for family fun

Exclusive holidays for young people or – 'it ain't what you do, it's who you do it with'

Feel free to join in as much or as little as you like

The freedom of your own holiday home

Choice locations from Corfu to Skiathos

Special offers on car hire

A LA CARTE

Hand-picked, top-class hotels

Taxi transfer from the airport

Flowers and wine on arrival

A choice of Cruise and Stay holidays

Small & Friendly

Smaller hotels, pensions and tavernas

Many family run, all easy going

Carefully selected for their friendly style

A choice of Mainland and Island resorts

A choice of 4 Greek Tours

Greek Mainland plus Crete and Rhodes

Tour and Stay options

Value-packed excursions included

Reliable, low cost flights

10 Greek destinations

11 UK airports